Learning Docker

Optimize the power of Docker to run your applications quickly and easily

Pethuru Raj

Jeeva S. Chelladhurai

Vinod Singh

BIRMINGHAM - MUMBAI

Learning Docker

First published: June 2015

Production reference: 1240615

Published by Packt Publishing Ltd.
Livery Place
35 Livery Street
Birmingham B3 2PB, UK.

ISBN 978-1-78439-793-7

www.packtpub.com

Credits

Authors
Pethuru Raj
Jeeva S. Chelladhurai
Vinod Singh

Reviewers
Shashikant Bangera
Sergei Vizel
Baohua Yang

Commissioning Editor
Sarah Crofton

Acquisition Editor
Larissa Pinto

Content Development Editor
Kirti Patil

Technical Editors
Dhiraj Chandanshive
Narsimha Pai

Copy Editors
Vikrant Phadke
Rashmi Sawant
Trishla Singh

Project Coordinator
Nidhi Joshi

Proofreader
Safis Editing

Indexer
Hemangini Bari

Graphics
Sheetal Aute

Production Coordinator
Nitesh Thakur

Cover Work
Nitesh Thakur

About the Authors

Pethuru Raj, PhD, works as a cloud architect at the IBM Global Cloud Center of Excellence (CoE) in Bangalore, India. He completed his CSIR-sponsored PhD degree at Anna University, Chennai, and continued his UGC-sponsored postdoctoral research at the Department of Computer Science and Automation of IISc, Bangalore. Thereafter, he was granted a couple of international research fellowships (JSPS and JST) to work as a research scientist for 3 years at two leading Japanese universities.

Pethuru has contributed to a number of high-quality technology books that are edited by internationally acclaimed professionals. In association with another IBMer, he has recently submitted the complete manuscript for a book called *Smart Cities: the Enabling Technologies and Tools*, to be published by the CRC Press in the USA in May 2015. He has collaborated with a few established authors to publish a book called *High-Performance Big Data Analytics*, which will be published by Springer-Verlag, UK, in 2015. He maintains an IT portal at http://www.peterindia.net, and his LinkedIn profile can be found at https://www.linkedin.com/in/peterindia.

Jeeva S. Chelladhurai has been working as a technical project manager at the IBM Global Cloud Center of Excellence (CoE) in India for the last 8 years. He has more than 18 years of experience in the IT industry. In various capacities, he has technically managed and mentored diverse teams across the globe in envisaging and building pioneering telecommunication products. He specializes in cloud solution delivery, with a focus on data center optimization, software-defined environments (SDEs), and distributed application development, deployment, and delivery using the newest Docker technology. Jeeva is also a strong proponent of Agile methodologies, DevOps, and IT automation. He holds a master's degree in computer science from Manonmaniam Sundaranar University and a graduation certificate in project management from Boston University. He has been instrumental in crafting reusable assets for IBM solution architects and consultants in Docker-inspired containerization technology.

Vinod Singh is a lead architect for IBM's cloud computing offerings. He has more than 18 years of experience in the cloud computing, networking, and data communication domains. Currently, he works for IBM's cloud application services and partner marketplace offerings. Vinod has worked on architecting, deploying, and running IBM's PaaS offering (BlueMix) on the SoftLayer infrastructure cloud. He also provides consultancy and advisory services to clients across the globe on the adoption of cloud technologies. He is currently focusing on various applications and services on the IBM Marketplace/BlueMix/SoftLayer platform. He is a graduate engineer from the National Institute of Technology, Jaipur, and completed his master's degree at BITS, Pilani.

About the Reviewers

Shashikant Bangera is a DevOps architect with 16 years of IT experience. He has vast exposure to DevOps tools across the platform, with core expertise in open source. He has helped his customers adopt DevOps practice and implemented Enterprise DevOps for them and has also contributed to many open sources platforms, such as DevOps Publication. He has designed an automated on-demand environment with a set of open source tools and also an environment booking tool, which is available on GitHuB. His Twitter handle is `@shzshi`.

Sergei Vizel is a senior software engineer at Modera (`modera.org`). He is a full-stack web application developer with more than 10 years of impressive experience. He is a firm believer of the value and power of open source software and contributes to projects on GitHub. Sergei has published numerous pieces of open source code of his own. You can learn more about him and contact him on GitHub via `https://github.com/cravler`.

Baohua Yang is a research scientist on cloud-computing-related technologies at IBM. He is a contributor to many open source communities such as OpenStack, OpenvSwitch, Docker, and OpenDaylight. He is also a TPC member and a reviewer of a number of international conferences and journals.

Baohua's interests mainly include system and application architecture, performance optimization, and security issues in cloud networking and distributed systems, especially in emerging technologies such as cloud computing, SDN, and NFV. He has written many technical books and articles to introduce and analyze these techniques. He loves open source technologies and enjoys designing and implementing efficient systems with elegant architecture.

www.PacktPub.com

Support files, eBooks, discount offers, and more

For support files and downloads related to your book, please visit www.PacktPub.com.

Did you know that Packt offers eBook versions of every book published, with PDF and ePub files available? You can upgrade to the eBook version at www.PacktPub.com and as a print book customer, you are entitled to a discount on the eBook copy. Get in touch with us at service@packtpub.com for more details.

At www.PacktPub.com, you can also read a collection of free technical articles, sign up for a range of free newsletters and receive exclusive discounts and offers on Packt books and eBooks.

https://www2.packtpub.com/books/subscription/packtlib

Do you need instant solutions to your IT questions? PacktLib is Packt's online digital book library. Here, you can search, access, and read Packt's entire library of books.

Why subscribe?

- Fully searchable across every book published by Packt
- Copy and paste, print, and bookmark content
- On demand and accessible via a web browser

Free access for Packt account holders

If you have an account with Packt at www.PacktPub.com, you can use this to access PacktLib today and view 9 entirely free books. Simply use your login credentials for immediate access.

Table of Contents

Preface

We have been fiddling with virtualization techniques and tools for quite a long time now in order to establish the much-demanded software portability. The inhibiting dependency factor between software and hardware needs to be decimated by leveraging virtualization, a kind of beneficial abstraction, through an additional layer of indirection. The idea is to run any software on any hardware. This is achieved by creating multiple virtual machines (VMs) out of a single physical server, with each VM having its own operating system (OS). Through this isolation, which is enacted through automated tools and controlled resource sharing, heterogeneous applications are accommodated in a physical machine.

With virtualization, IT infrastructures become open, programmable, remotely monitorable, manageable, and maintainable. Business workloads can be hosted in appropriately-sized virtual machines and delivered to the outside world, ensuring broader and more frequent utilization. On the other hand, for high-performance applications, virtual machines across multiple physical machines can be readily identified and rapidly combined to guarantee any kind of high-performance requirement.

The virtualization paradigm has its own drawbacks. Because of the verbosity and bloatedness (every VM carries its own operating system), VM provisioning typically takes a while, the performance goes down due to excessive usage of computational resources, and so on. Furthermore, the growing need for portability is not fully met by virtualization. Hypervisor software from different vendors comes in the way of ensuring application portability. Differences in the OS and application distributions, versions, editions, and patches hinder smooth portability. Computer virtualization has flourished, whereas the other, closely associated concepts of network and storage virtualization are just taking off. Building distributed applications through VM interactions invites and involves some practical difficulties.

Let's move on to containerization. All of these barriers contribute to the unprecedented success of the idea of containerization. A container generally contains an application, and all of the application's libraries, binaries, and other dependencies are stuffed together to be presented as a comprehensive, yet compact, entity for the outside world. Containers are exceptionally lightweight, highly portable, easily and quickly provisionable, and so on. Docker containers achieve native system performance. The greatly articulated DevOps goal gets fully fulfilled through application containers. As best practice, it is recommended that every container hosts one application or service.

The popular Docker containerization platform has come up with an enabling engine to simplify and accelerate the life cycle management of containers. There are industry-strength and openly automated tools made freely available to facilitate the needs of container networking and orchestration. Therefore , producing and sustaining business-critical distributed applications is becoming easy. Business workloads are methodically containerized to be easily taken to cloud environments, and they are exposed for container crafters and composers to bring forth cloud-based software solutions and services. Precisely speaking, containers are turning out to be the most featured, favored, and fine-tuned runtime environment for IT and business services.

This book is meticulously designed and developed in order to empower developers, cloud architects, business managers, and strategists with all the right and relevant information on the Docker platform and its capacity to power up mission-critical, composite, and distributed applications across industry verticals.

What this book covers

Chapter 1, *Getting Started with Docker*, talks about the Docker platform and how it simplifies and speeds up the process of realizing containerized workloads to be readily deployed and run on a variety of platforms. This chapter also has step-by-step details on installing the Docker engine, downloading a Docker image from the centralized Docker Hub, creating a Docker container out of that image, and troubleshooting the Docker container.

Chapter 2, *Handling Docker Containers*, is primarily meant to expound the commands required to manage Docker images and containers. This chapter provides the basic Docker terminologies needed to understand the output of Docker commands. Other details covered here include starting an interactive session inside a container, managing your images, running containers, and tracking changes inside containers.

Chapter 3, *Building Images*, introduces Docker's integrated image building system. The other important topics covered in this chapter include a quick overview of a Dockerfile's syntax and a bit of theory on how Docker stores images.

Chapter 4, Publishing Images, focuses on publishing images on the centralized Docker Hub and how to get the most out of the Docker Hub. The other important contents in the chapter include greater details about the Docker Hub, how to push images to the Docker Hub, the automatic building of images, creating organizations on Docker Hub, and finally private repositories.

Chapter 5, Running Your Private Docker Infrastructure, explains how corporates can set up their own private repositories. Due to certain reasons, corporates may not want to host specific Docker images in publicly-available image repositories, such as the Docker Hub. Here, the need for their own private repository to keep up those images arises. This chapter has all of the information required to set up and sustain private repositories.

Chapter 6, Running Services in a Container, illustrates how a web application can be run inside a Docker container as a service, and how to expose the service for the outside world to find and access it. How the appropriate Dockerfile gets developed to simplify this task is also described in detail.

Chapter 7, Sharing Data with Containers, shows you how to use Docker's volumes feature to share data between the Docker host and its containers. The other topics covered here are how to share data between containers, the common use cases, and the typical pitfalls to avoid.

Chapter 8, Orchestrating Containers, focuses on orchestrating multiple containers towards composite, containerized workloads. It is a well-known truth that orchestration plays a major role in producing composite applications. This chapter includes some information about orchestration and the toolset made available for enabling the process of orchestration. Finally, you will find a well-orchestrated example of how containers can be orchestrated to bring forth highly reusable and business-aware containers.

Chapter 9, Testing with Docker, focuses on testing your code inside Docker images. In this chapter, you find out how to run the tests inside an ad hoc Docker image. Finally, you come across details of how to integrate Docker testing into a continuous integration server, such as Jenkins.

Chapter 10, Debugging Containers, teaches you how to debug applications running inside containers. Also, the details regarding how Docker ensures that processes running inside containers are isolated from the outside world are covered. Furthermore, descriptions of the usage of the nsenter and nsinit tools for effective debugging are included.

Chapter 11, Securing Docker Containers, is crafted to explain the brewing security and privacy challenges and concerns, and how they are addressed through the liberal usage of competent standards, technologies, and tools. This chapter inscribes the mechanism on dropping user privileges inside an image. There is also a brief introduction on how the security capabilities introduced in SELinux come in handy when securing Docker containers.

What you need for this book

The Docker platform requires a 64-bit hardware system to run on. Docker applications have been developed on Ubuntu 14.04 for this book, but this does not mean that the Docker platform cannot run on other Linux distributions, such as Redhat, CentOS, CoreOS, and so on. However, the Linux kernel version must be 3.10 or above.

Who this book is for

If you are an application developer who wants to learn about Docker in order to utilize its features for application deployment, then this book is for you. No prior knowledge of Docker is required.

Conventions

In this book, you will find a number of text styles that distinguish between different kinds of information. Here are some examples of these styles and an explanation of their meaning.

Code words in text, database table names, folder names, filenames, file extensions, pathnames, dummy URLs, user input, and Twitter handles are shown as follows: "If the docker service is running, then this command will print the status as start/running, along with its process ID."

A block of code is set as follows:

```
FROM busybox:latest
CMD echo Hello World!!
```

Any command-line input or output is written as follows:

```
$ sudo docker tag 224affbf9a65localhost:5000/vinoddandy/
dockerfileimageforhub
```

New terms and **important words** are shown in bold. Words that you see on the screen, for example, in menus or dialog boxes, appear in the text like this: "Select the **Docker** option, which is in the drop-down menu, and then click on **Launch Now**."

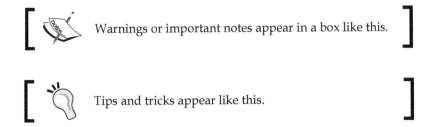

Warnings or important notes appear in a box like this.

Tips and tricks appear like this.

Reader feedback

Feedback from our readers is always welcome. Let us know what you think about this book—what you liked or disliked. Reader feedback is important for us as it helps us develop titles that you will really get the most out of.

To send us general feedback, simply e-mail feedback@packtpub.com, and mention the book's title in the subject of your message.

If there is a topic that you have expertise in and you are interested in either writing or contributing to a book, see our author guide at www.packtpub.com/authors.

Customer support

Now that you are the proud owner of a Packt book, we have a number of things to help you to get the most from your purchase.

Downloading the example code

You can download the example code files from your account at http://www.packtpub.com for all the Packt Publishing books you have purchased. If you purchased this book elsewhere, you can visit http://www.packtpub.com/support and register to have the files e-mailed directly to you.

Errata

Although we have taken every care to ensure the accuracy of our content, mistakes do happen. If you find a mistake in one of our books—maybe a mistake in the text or the code—we would be grateful if you could report this to us. By doing so, you can save other readers from frustration and help us improve subsequent versions of this book. If you find any errata, please report them by visiting `http://www.packtpub.com/submit-errata`, selecting your book, clicking on the **Errata Submission Form** link, and entering the details of your errata. Once your errata are verified, your submission will be accepted and the errata will be uploaded to our website or added to any list of existing errata under the Errata section of that title.

To view the previously submitted errata, go to `https://www.packtpub.com/books/content/support` and enter the name of the book in the search field. The required information will appear under the **Errata** section.

Piracy

Piracy of copyrighted material on the Internet is an ongoing problem across all media. At Packt, we take the protection of our copyright and licenses very seriously. If you come across any illegal copies of our works in any form on the Internet, please provide us with the location address or website name immediately so that we can pursue a remedy.

Please contact us at `copyright@packtpub.com` with a link to the suspected pirated material.

We appreciate your help in protecting our authors and our ability to bring you valuable content.

Questions

If you have a problem with any aspect of this book, you can contact us at `questions@packtpub.com`, and we will do our best to address the problem.

1
Getting Started with Docker

These days, Docker technology is gaining more market and more mind shares among information technology (IT) professionals across the globe. In this chapter, we would like to shed more light on Docker, and show why it is being touted as the next best thing for the impending cloud IT era. In order to make this book relevant to software engineers, we have listed the steps needed for crafting highly usable application-aware containers, registering them in a public registry repository, and then deploying them in multiple IT environments (on-premises as well as off-premises). In this book, we have clearly explained the prerequisites and the most important details of Docker, with the help of all the education and experiences that we could gain through a series of careful implementations of several useful Docker containers in different systems. For doing this, we used our own laptops as well as a few leading public **Cloud Service Providers (CSP)**.

We would like to introduce you to the practical side of Docker for the game-changing Docker-inspired containerization movement.

In this chapter, we will cover the following topics:

- An introduction to Docker
- Docker on Linux
- Differentiating between containerization and virtualization
- Installing the Docker engine
- Understanding the Docker setup
- Downloading the first image
- Running the first container
- Running a Docker container on **Amazon Web Services (AWS)**
- Troubleshooting the Docker containers

An introduction to Docker

Due to its overwhelming usage across industry verticals, the IT domain has been stuffed with many new and pathbreaking technologies used not only for bringing in more decisive automation but also for overcoming existing complexities. Virtualization has set the goal of bringing forth IT infrastructure optimization and portability. However, virtualization technology has serious drawbacks, such as performance degradation due to the heavyweight nature of **virtual machines (VM)**, the lack of application portability, slowness in provisioning of IT resources, and so on. Therefore, the IT industry has been steadily embarking on a Docker-inspired containerization journey. The Docker initiative has been specifically designed for making the containerization paradigm easier to grasp and use. Docker enables the containerization process to be accomplished in a risk-free and accelerated fashion.

Precisely speaking, **Docker** is an open source containerization engine, which automates the packaging, shipping, and deployment of any software applications that are presented as lightweight, portable, and self-sufficient containers, that will run virtually anywhere.

A Docker **container** is a software bucket comprising everything necessary to run the software independently. There can be multiple Docker containers in a single machine and containers are completely isolated from one another as well as from the host machine.

In other words, a Docker container includes a software component along with all of its dependencies (binaries, libraries, configuration files, scripts, jars, and so on). Therefore, the Docker containers could be fluently run on x64 Linux kernel supporting namespaces, control groups, and file systems, such as **Another Union File System (AUFS)**. However, as indicated in this chapter, there are pragmatic workarounds for running Docker on other mainstream operating systems, such as Windows, Mac, and so on. The Docker container has its own process space and network interface. It can also run things as root, and have its own `/sbin/init`, which can be different from the host machines'.

In a nutshell, the Docker solution lets us quickly assemble composite, enterprise-scale, and business-critical applications. For doing this, we can use different and distributed software components: Containers eliminate the friction that comes with shipping code to distant locations. Docker also lets us test the code and then deploy it in production as fast as possible. The Docker solution primarily consists of the following components:

- The Docker engine
- The Docker Hub

The Docker engine is for enabling the realization of purpose-specific as well as generic Docker containers. The Docker Hub is a fast-growing repository of the Docker images that can be combined in different ways for producing publicly findable, network-accessible, and widely usable containers.

Docker on Linux

Suppose that we want to directly run the containers on a Linux machine. The Docker engine produces, monitors, and manages multiple containers as illustrated in the following diagram:

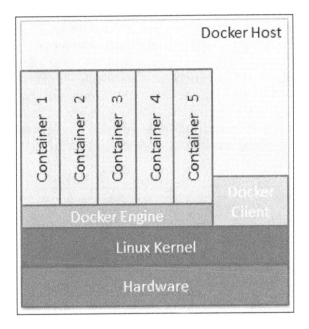

The preceding diagram vividly illustrates how future IT systems would have hundreds of application-aware containers, which would innately be capable of facilitating their seamless integration and orchestration for deriving modular applications (business, social, mobile, analytical, and embedded solutions). These contained applications could fluently run on converged, federated, virtualized, shared, dedicated, and automated infrastructures.

Differentiating between containerization and virtualization

It is pertinent, and paramount to extract and expound the game-changing advantages of the Docker-inspired containerization movement over the widely used and fully matured virtualization paradigm. In the containerization paradigm, strategically sound optimizations have been accomplished through a few crucial and well-defined rationalizations and the insightful sharing of the compute resources. Some of the innate and hitherto underutilized capabilities of the Linux kernel have been rediscovered. These capabilities have been rewarded for bringing in much-wanted automation and acceleration, which will enable the fledgling containerization idea to reach greater heights in the days ahead, especially those of the cloud era. The noteworthy business and technical advantages of these include the bare metal-scale performance, real-time scalability, higher availability, and so on. All the unwanted bulges and flab are being sagaciously eliminated to speed up the roll-out of hundreds of application containers in seconds and to reduce the time taken for marketing and valuing in a cost-effective fashion. The following diagram on the left-hand side depicts the virtualization aspect, whereas the diagram on the right-hand side vividly illustrates the simplifications that are being achieved in the containers:

The following table gives a direct comparison between virtual machines and containers:

Virtual Machines (VMs)	Containers
Represents hardware-level virtualization	Represents operating system virtualization
Heavyweight	Lightweight
Slow provisioning	Real-time provisioning and scalability
Limited performance	Native performance
Fully isolated and hence more secure	Process-level isolation and hence less secure

The convergence of containerization and virtualization

A hybrid model, having features from both the virtual machines and that of containers, is being developed. It is the emergence of system containers, as illustrated in the preceding right-hand-side diagram. Traditional hypervisors, which implicitly represent hardware virtualization, directly secure the environment with the help of the server hardware. That is, VMs are completely isolated from the other VMs as well as from the underlying system. But for containers, this isolation happens at the process level and hence, they are liable for any kind of security incursion. Furthermore, some vital features that are available in the VMs are not available in the containers. For instance, there is no support for SSH, TTY, and the other security functionalities in the containers. On the other hand, VMs are resource-hungry and hence, their performance gets substantially degraded. Indeed, in containerization parlance, the overhead of a classic hypervisor and a guest operating system will be eliminated to achieve bare metal performance. Therefore, a few VMs can be provisioned and made available to work on a single machine. Thus, on one hand, we have the fully isolated VMs with average performance and on the other side, we have the containers that lack some of the key features, but are blessed with high performance. Having understood the ensuing needs, product vendors are working on system containers. The objective of this new initiative is to provide full system containers with the performance that you would expect from bare metal servers, but with the experience of virtual machines. The system containers in the preceding right-hand-side diagram represent the convergence of two important concepts (virtualization and containerization) for smarter IT. We will hear and read more about this blending in the future.

Containerization technologies

Having recognized the role and the relevance of the containerization paradigm for IT infrastructure augmentation and acceleration, a few technologies that leverage the unique and decisive impacts of the containerization idea have come into existence and they have been enumerated as follows:

- **LXC (Linux Containers)**: This is the father of all kinds of containers and it represents an operating-system-level virtualization environment for running multiple isolated Linux systems (containers) on a single Linux machine.

  The article *LXC* on the Wikipedia website states that:

  > "*The Linux kernel provides the cgroups functionality that allows limitation and prioritization of resources (CPU, memory, block I/O, network, etc.) without the need for starting any virtual machines, and namespace isolation functionality that allows complete isolation of an applications' view of the operating environment, including process trees, networking, user IDs and mounted file systems.*"

  You can get more information from `http://en.wikipedia.org/wiki/LXC`.

- **OpenVZ**: This is an OS-level virtualization technology based on the Linux kernel and the operating system. OpenVZ allows a physical server to run multiple isolated operating system instances, called containers, virtual private servers (VPSs), or virtual environments (VEs).

- **The FreeBSD jail**: This is a mechanism that implements an OS-level virtualization, which lets the administrators partition a FreeBSD-based computer system into several independent mini-systems called *jails*.

- **The AIX Workload partitions (WPARs)**: These are the software implementations of the OS-level virtualization technology, which provide application environment isolation and resource control.

- **Solaris Containers** (including **Solaris Zones**): This is an implementation of the OS-level virtualization technology for the x86 and SPARC systems. A Solaris Container is a combination of the system resource controls and boundary separation provided by *zones*. Zones act as completely isolated virtual servers within a single operating system instance.

In this book, considering the surging popularity and the mass adoption happening to Docker, we have chosen to dig deeper, dwell in detail on the Docker platform, the one-stop solution for the simplified and streamlined containerization movement.

Installing the Docker engine

The Docker engine is built on top of the Linux kernel and it extensively leverages its features. Therefore, at this point in time, the Docker engine can only be directly run on Linux OS distributions. Nonetheless, the Docker engine could be run on the Mac and Microsoft Windows operating systems by using the lightweight Linux VMs with the help of adapters, such as Boot2Docker. Due to the surging growing of Docker, it is now being packaged by all major Linux distributions so that they can retain their loyal users as well as attract new users. You can install the Docker engine by using the corresponding packaging tool of the Linux distribution; for example, by using the apt-get command for Debian and Ubuntu, and the yum command for RedHat, Fedora, and CentOS.

 We have chosen the *Ubuntu Trusty 14.04 (LTS) (64-bit)* Linux distribution for all practical purposes.

Installing from the Ubuntu package repository

This section explains the steps involved in installing the Docker engine from the Ubuntu package repository in detail. At the time of writing this book, the Ubuntu repository had packaged Docker 1.0.1, whereas the latest version of Docker was 1.5. We strongly recommend installing Docker version 1.5 or greater by using any one of the methods described in the next section.

However, if for any reason you have to install the Ubuntu packaged version, then please follow the steps described here:

1. The best practice for installing the Ubuntu packaged version is to begin the installation process by resynchronizing with the Ubuntu package repository. This step will essentially update the package repository to the latest published packages, thus we will ensure that we always get the latest published version by using the command shown here:

   ```
   $ sudo apt-get update
   ```

 Downloading the example code

You can download the example code files from your account at http://www.packtpub.com for all the Packt Publishing books you have purchased. If you purchased this book elsewhere, you can visit http://www.packtpub.com/support and register to have the files e-mailed directly to you.

2. Kick-start the installation by using the following command. This setup will install the Docker engine along with a few more support files, and it will also start the docker service instantaneously:

```
$ sudo apt-get install -y docker.io
```

 The Docker package is called docker.io because an older version of the Ubuntu package was called docker. As a result, all the files with the name docker are installed as docker.io.

Examples are /usr/bin/docker.io and /etc/bash_completion.d/docker.io.

3. For your convenience, you can create a soft link for docker.io called docker. This will enable you to execute Docker commands as docker instead of docker.io. You can do this by using the following command:

```
$ sudo ln -sf /usr/bin/docker.io /usr/local/bin/docker
```

 The official Ubuntu package does not come with the latest stable version of docker.

Installing the latest Docker using docker.io script

The official distributions might not package the latest version of Docker. In such a case, you can install the latest version of Docker either manually or by using the automated scripts provided by the Docker community.

For installing the latest version of Docker manually, follow these steps:

1. Add the Docker release tool's repository path to your APT sources, as shown here:

```
$ sudo sh -c "echo deb https://get.docker.io/ubuntu \
    docker main > /etc/apt/sources.list.d/docker.list"
```

2. Import the Docker release tool's public key by running the following command:

```
$ sudo apt-key adv --keyserver \
    hkp://keyserver.ubuntu.com:80 --recv-keys \
    36A1D7869245C8950F966E92D8576A8BA88D21E9
```

3. Resynchronize with the package repository by using the command shown here:

```
$ sudo apt-get update
```

4. Install `docker` and then start the `docker` service.

```
$ sudo apt-get install -y lxc-docker
```

 The `lxc-docker` command will install the Docker image using the name `docker`.

The Docker community has taken a step forward by hiding these details in an automated install script. This script enables the installation of Docker on most of the popular Linux distributions, either through the `curl` command or through the `wget` command, as shown here:

- For curl command:

  ```
  $ sudo curl -sSL https://get.docker.io/ | sh
  ```

- For wget command:

  ```
  $ sudo wget -qO- https://get.docker.io/ | sh
  ```

 The preceding automated script approach enforces AUFS as the underlying Docker file system. This script probes the AUFS driver, and then installs it automatically if it is not found in the system. In addition, it also conducts some basic tests upon installation for verifying the sanity.

Understanding the Docker setup

It's important to understand Docker's components and their versions, storage, execution drivers, file locations, and so on. Incidentally, the quest for understanding the Docker setup would also reveal whether the installation was successful or not. You can accomplish this by using two `docker` subcommands, namely `docker version`, and `docker info`.

Let's start our docker journey with the docker version subcommand, as shown here:

```
$ sudo docker version
Client version: 1.5.0
Client API version: 1.17
Go version (client): go1.4.1
Git commit (client): a8a31ef
OS/Arch (client): linux/amd64
Server version: 1.5.0
Server API version: 1.17
Go version (server): go1.4.1
Git commit (server): a8a31ef
```

Although the docker version subcommand lists many lines of text, as a Docker user, you should know what these following output lines mean:

- The client version
- The client API version
- The server version
- The server API version

The client and server versions that have been considered here are 1.5.0 and the client API and the server API, versions 1.17.

If we dissect the internals of the docker version subcommand, then it will first list the client-related information that is stored locally. Subsequently, it will make a REST API call to the server over HTTP to obtain the server-related details.

Let's learn more about the Docker environment using the docker info subcommand:

```
$ sudo docker -D info
Containers: 0
Images: 0
Storage Driver: aufs
```

```
Root Dir: /var/lib/docker/aufs

Backing Filesystem: extfs

Dirs: 0

Execution Driver: native-0.2

Kernel Version: 3.13.0-45-generic

Operating System: Ubuntu 14.04.1 LTS

CPUs: 4

Total Memory: 3.908 GiB

Name: dockerhost

ID: ZNXR:QQSY:IGKJ:ZLYU:G4P7:AXVC:2KAJ:A3Q5:YCRQ:IJD3:7RON:IJ6Y

Debug mode (server): false

Debug mode (client): true

Fds: 10

Goroutines: 14

EventsListeners: 0

Init Path: /usr/bin/docker

Docker Root Dir: /var/lib/docker

WARNING: No swap limit support
```

As you can see in the output of a freshly installed Docker engine, the number of Containers and Images is invariably nil. The Storage Driver has been set up as aufs, and the directory has been given the /var/lib/docker/aufs location. The Execution Driver has been set to the native mode. This command also lists details, such as the Kernel Version, the Operating System, the number of CPUs, the Total Memory, and Name, the new Docker hostname.

Client server communication

On Linux installations, Docker is usually programmed for carrying out server-client communication by using the Unix socket (/var/run/docker.sock). Docker also has an IANA registered port, which is 2375. However, for security reasons, this port is not enabled by default.

Downloading the first Docker image

Having installed the Docker engine successfully, the next logical step is to download the images from the Docker registry. The Docker registry is an application repository, which hosts a range of applications that vary between basic Linux images and advanced applications. The `docker pull` subcommand is used for downloading any number of images from the registry. In this section, we will download a tiny version of Linux called the `busybox` image by using the following command:

```
$ sudo docker pull busybox
511136ea3c5a: Pull complete
df7546f9f060: Pull complete
ea13149945cb: Pull complete
4986bf8c1536: Pull complete
busybox:latest: The image you are pulling has been verified. Important:
image verification is a tech preview feature and should not be relied on
to provide security.
Status: Downloaded newer image for busybox:latest
```

Once the images have been downloaded, they can be verified by using the `docker images` subcommand, as shown here:

```
$ sudo docker images
REPOSITORY      TAG       IMAGE ID        CREATED        VIRTUAL SIZE
busybox         latest    4986bf8c1536    12 weeks ago 2.433 MB
```

Running the first Docker container

Now, you can start your first Docker container. It is standard practice to start with the basic *Hello World!* application. In the following example, we will echo `Hello World!` by using a `busybox` image, which we have already downloaded, as shown here:

```
$ sudo docker run busybox echo "Hello World!"
"Hello World!"
```

Cool, isn't it? You have set up your first Docker container in no time. In the preceding example, the `docker run` subcommand has been used for creating a container and for printing `Hello World!` by using the `echo` command.

Running a Docker container on Amazon Web Services

Amazon Web Services (AWS) announced the availability of Docker containers at the beginning of 2014, as a part of its Elastic Beanstalk offering. At the end of 2014, they revolutionized Docker deployment and provided the users with options shown here for running Docker containers:

- The Amazon EC2 container service (only available in **preview** mode at the time of writing this book)
- Docker deployment by using the Amazon Elastic Beans services

The Amazon EC2 container service lets you start and stop the container-enabled applications with the help of simple API calls. AWS has introduced the concept of a cluster for viewing the state of your containers. You can view the tasks from a centralized service, and it gives you access to many familiar Amazon EC2 features, such as the security groups, the EBS volumes and the IAM roles.

Please note that this service is still not available in the AWS console. You need to install AWS CLI on your machine to deploy, run, and access this service.

The AWS Elastic Beanstalk service supports the following:

- A single container that supports Elastic Beanstalk by using a console. Currently, it supports the PHP and Python applications.
- A single container that supports Elastic Beanstalk by using a command line tool called *eb*. It supports the same PHP and Python applications.
- Use of multiple container environments by using Elastic beanstalk.

Currently, AWS supports the latest Docker version, which is 1.5.

This section provides a step-by-step process to deploy a sample application on a Docker container running on AWS Elastic Beanstalk.The following are the steps of deployment:

1. Log in to the AWS Elastic Beanstalk console by using this `https://console.aws.amazon.com/elasticbeanstalk/` URL.
2. Select a region where you want to deploy your application, as shown here:

3. Select the **Docker** option, which is in the drop down menu, and then click on **Launch Now**. The next screen will be shown after a few minutes, as shown here:

Now, click on the URL that is next to **Default-Environment (Default-Environment-pjgerbmmjm.elasticbeanstalk.com)**, as shown here:

Troubleshooting

Most of the time, you will not encounter any issues when installing Docker. However, unplanned failures might occur. Therefore, it is necessary to discuss prominent troubleshooting techniques and tips. Let's begin by discussing the troubleshooting knowhow in this section. The first tip is that the running status of Docker should be checked by using the following command:

```
$ sudo service docker status
```

However, if Docker has been installed by using the Ubuntu package, then you will have to use docker.io as the service name. If the docker service is running, then this command will print the status as start/running along with its process ID.

If you are still experiencing issues with the Docker setup, then you could open the Docker log by using the /var/log/upstart/docker.log file for further investigation.

Summary

Containerization is going to be a dominant and decisive paradigm for the enterprise as well as cloud IT environments in the future because of its hitherto unforeseen automation and acceleration capabilities. There are several mechanisms in place for taking the containerization movement to greater heights. However, Docker has zoomed ahead of everyone in this hot race, and it has successfully decimated the previously-elucidated barriers.

In this chapter, we have exclusively concentrated on the practical side of Docker for giving you a head start in learning about the most promising technology. We have listed the appropriate steps and tips for effortlessly installing the Docker engine in different environments, for leveraging and for building, installing, and running a few sample Docker containers, both in local as well as remote environments. We will dive deep into the world of Docker and dig deeper to extract and share tactically and strategically sound information with you in the ensuing chapters. Please read on to gain the required knowledge about advanced topics, such as container integration, orchestration, management, governance, security, and so on, through the Docker engine. We will also discuss a bevy of third-party tools.

Handling Docker Containers

2

In the previous chapter, we explained stimulating and sustainable concepts, which showed the Docker's way of crafting futuristic and flexible application-aware containers. We discussed all the relevant details of producing the Docker containers in multiple environments (on-premise as well as off-premise). Using these techniques, you can easily replicate these features in your own environments to get a rewarding experience. Therefore, the next step for us is to understand the container's life cycle aspects in a decisive manner. You will learn the optimal utilization of containers of our own as well as those of other third-party containers in an effective and risk-free way. Containers are to be found, assessed, accessed, and leveraged toward bigger and better applications. There are several tools that have emerged to streamline the handling of containers.

In this chapter, we will dig deeper and describe the critical aspects of container handling at length. A number of practical tips and execution commands for the leveraging of containers will also be discussed in this chapter.

In this chapter, we will cover the following topics:

- Clarifying the Docker terms
- Working with the Docker images and containers
- The meaning of the Docker registry and its repository
- The Docker Hub Registry
- Searching the Docker images
- Working with an interactive container
- Tracking the changes inside the containers
- Controlling and housekeeping the Docker containers
- Building images from containers
- Launching a container as a daemon

Clarifying the Docker terms

To make this chapter substantially simpler to understand and to minimize any kind of ambiguity, the frequently used terms will be explained in the following section.

Docker images and containers

A **Docker image** is a collection of all of the files that make up a software application. Each change that is made to the original image is stored in a separate layer. To be precise, any Docker image has to originate from a base image according to the various requirements. Additional modules can be attached to the base image for deriving the various images that can exhibit the preferred behavior. Each time you commit to a Docker image you are creating a new layer on the Docker image, but the original image and each pre-existing layer remains unchanged. In other words, images are typically of the read-only type. If they are empowered through the systematic attachment of newer modules, then a fresh image will be created with a new name. The Docker images are turning out to be a viable base for developing and deploying the Docker containers.

A base image has been illustrated here. Debian is the base image, and a variety of desired capabilities in the form of functional modules can be incorporated on the base image for arriving at multiple images:

Every image has a unique ID, as explained in the following section. The base images can be enhanced such that they can create the parent images, which in turn can be used for creating the child images. The base image does not have any parent, that is, the parent images sit on top of the base image. When we work with an image and if we don't specify that image through an appropriate identity (say, a new name), then the latest image (recently generated) will always be identified and used by the Docker engine.

As per the Docker home page, a Docker image has a read-only template. For example, an image could contain an Ubuntu operating system, with Apache and your web application installed on it. Docker provides a simple way for building new images or of updating the existing images. You can also download the Docker images that the other people have already created. The Docker images are the building components of the Docker containers. In general, the base Docker image represents an operating system, and in the case of Linux, the base image can be one of its distributions, such as Debian. Adding additional modules to the base image ultimately dawns a container. The easiest way of thinking about a container is as the read-write layer that sits on one or more read-only images. When the container is run, the Docker engine not only merges all of the required images together, but it also merges the changes from the read-write layer into the container itself. This makes it a self-contained, extensible, and executable system. The changes can be merged by using the Docker docker commit subcommand. The new container will accommodate all the changes that are made to the base image. The new image will form a new layer on top of the base image.

The following diagram will tell you everything clearly. The base image is the **Debian** distribution, then there is an addition of two images (the **emacs** and the **Apache** server), and this will result in the container:

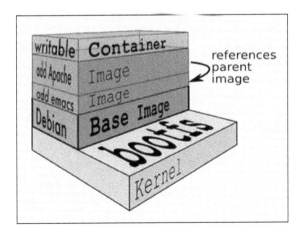

Each commit invariably makes a new image. This makes the number of images go up steadily, and so managing them becomes a complicated affair. However, the storage space is not a big challenge because the new image that is generated is only comprised of the newly added modules. In a way, this is similar to the popular object storage in the cloud environments. Every time you update an object, there will be a new object that gets created with the latest modification and then it is stored with a new ID. In the case of object storage, the storage size balloons significantly.

A Docker layer

A **Docker layer** could represent either read-only images or read-write images. However, the top layer of a container stack is always the read-write (writable) layer, which hosts a Docker container.

A Docker container

From the preceding diagram, it is clear that the read-write layer is the container layer. There could be several read-only images beneath the container layer. Typically, a container originates from a read-only image through the act of a commit. When you start a container, you actually refer to an image through its unique ID. Docker pulls the required image and its parent image. It continues to pull all the parent images until it reaches the base image.

Docker Registry

A **Docker Registry** is a place where the Docker images can be stored in order to be publicly found, accessed, and used by the worldwide developers for quickly crafting fresh and composite applications without any risks. Because all the stored images would have gone through multiple validations, verifications, and refinements, the quality of those images will be really high. Using the Docker push command, you can dispatch your Docker image to the Registry so that it is registered and deposited. As a clarification, the registry is for registering the Docker images, whereas the repository is for storing those registered Docker images in a publicly discoverable and centralized place. A Docker image is stored within a Repository in the Docker Registry. Each Repository is unique for each user or account.

Docker Repository

A **Docker Repository** is a namespace that is used for storing a Docker image. For instance, if your app is named `helloworld` and your username or namespace for the Registry is `thedockerbook` then, in the Docker Repository, where this image would be stored in the Docker Registry would be named `thedockerbook/helloworld`.

The base images are stored in the Docker Repository. The base images are the fountainheads for realizing the bigger and better images with the help of a careful addition of new modules. The child images are the ones that have their own parent images. The base image does not have any parent image. The images sitting on a base image are named as parent images because the parent images bear the child images.

Working with Docker images

In the previous chapter, we demonstrated the typical `Hello World!` example by using a `busybox` image. Now there is a need for a close observation of the output of the `docker pull` subcommand, which is a standard command for downloading the Docker images. You would have noticed the presence of the `busybox:latest` text in the output text, and we will explain this mystery in a detailed manner by bringing in a small twist to the `docker pull` subcommand by adding the `-a` option, as shown here:

```
$ sudo docker pull -a busybox
```

Surprisingly, you will observe that the Docker engine downloads a few more images with the `-a` option. You can easily check the images that are available on the Docker host by running the `docker images` subcommand, which comes in handy, and it reveals more details with respect to `:latest` and the additional images that are downloaded by running this command. Let us run this command:

```
$ sudo docker images
```

You will get the list of images, as follows:

```
REPOSITORY TAG                        IMAGE ID        CREATED
VIRTUAL SIZE
busybox      ubuntu-14.04             f6169d24347d    3 months ago   5.609
MB
busybox      ubuntu-12.04             492dad4279ba    3 months ago   5.455
MB
busybox      buildroot-2014.02        4986bf8c1536    3 months ago   2.433
MB
busybox      latest                   4986bf8c1536    3 months ago   2.433
MB
busybox      buildroot-2013.08.1      2aed48a4e41d    3 months ago   2.489
MB
```

Evidently, we have five items in the preceding list, and to gain a better understanding of those, we need to comprehend the information that is printed out by the Docker images subcommand. Here is a list of the possible categories:

- REPOSITORY: This is the name of the repository or image. In the preceding example, the repository name is busybox.

- TAG: This is the tag associated with the image, for example buildroot-2014.02, ubuntu-14.04, latest. One or more tags can be associated with one image.

 The ubuntu-* tagged images are built by using the busybox-static Ubuntu package and the buildroot-* tagged images are built from scratch by using the buildroot tool-chain.

- IMAGE ID: Every image is associated with a unique ID. The image ID is represented by using a 64 Hex digit long random number. By default, the Docker images subcommand will only show 12 Hex digits. You can display all the 64 Hex digits by using the --no-trunc flag (for example: sudo docker images --no-trunc).

- CREATED: Indicates the time when the image was created.

- VIRTUAL SIZE: Highlights the virtual size of the image.

You might be wondering how, in the preceding example, a single `pull` command with the `-a` option was able to download five images, even though we had only specified one image by the name of `busybox`. This happened because each Docker image repository can have multiple variants of the same image and the `-a` option downloads all the variants that are associated with that image. In the preceding example, the variants are tagged as `buildroot-2013.08.1`, `ubuntu-14.04`, `ubuntu-12.04`, `buildroot-2014.02` and `latest`. A closer observation of the image IDs will reveal that both `buildroot-2014.02` and `latest` share the image ID `4986bf8c1536`.

By default, Docker always uses the image that is tagged as `latest`. Each image variant can be directly identified by qualifying it with its tag. An image can be tag-qualified by appending the tag to the repository name with a `:` that is added between the tag and the repository name (`<repository>:<tag>`). For instance, you can launch a container with the `busybox:ubuntu-14.04` tag, as shown here:

```
$ sudo docker run -t -i busybox:ubuntu-14.04
```

The `docker pull` subcommand will always download the image variant that has the `latest` tag in that repository. However, if you choose to download an image variant other than the latest, then you can do so by qualifying your image with the tag name by using the following command:

```
$ sudo docker pull busybox:ubuntu-14.04
```

Docker Hub Registry

In the previous section, when you ran the `docker pull` subcommand, the `busybox` image got downloaded mysteriously. In this section, let's unravel the mystery around the `docker pull` subcommand and how the Docker Hub immensely contributed toward this unintended success.

The good folks in the Docker community have built a repository of images and they have made it publicly available at a default location, `index.docker.io`. This default location is called the Docker index. The `docker pull` subcommand is programmed to look for the images at this location. Therefore, when you `pull` a `busybox` image, it is effortlessly downloaded from the default registry. This mechanism helps in speeding up the spinning of the Docker containers. The Docker Index is the official repository that contains all the painstakingly curated images that are created and deposited by the worldwide Docker development community.

This so-called cure is enacted to ensure that all the images stored in the Docker index are secure and safe through a host of quarantine tasks. There are proven verification and validation methods for cleaning up any knowingly or unknowingly introduced malware, adware, viruses, and so on, from these Docker images. The digital signature is a prominent mechanism of the utmost integrity of the Docker images. Nonetheless, if the official image has been either corrupted, or tampered with, then the Docker engine will issue a warning and then continue to run the image.

In addition to the official repository, the Docker Hub Registry also provides a platform for the third-party developers and providers for sharing their images for general consumption. The third-party images are prefixed by the user ID of their developers or depositors. For example, `thedockerbook/helloworld` is a third-party image, wherein `thedockerbook` is the user ID and `helloworld` is the image repository name. You can download any third-party image by using the `docker pull` subcommand, as shown here:

```
$ sudo docker pull thedockerbook/helloworld
```

Apart from the preceding repository, the Docker ecosystem also provides a mechanism for leveraging the images from any third-party repository hub other than the Docker Hub Registry, and it provides the images hosted by the local repository hubs. As mentioned earlier, the Docker engine has been programmed to look for images in `index.docker.io` by default, whereas in the case of the third-party or the local repository hub, we must manually specify the path from where the image should be pulled. A manual repository path is similar to a URL without a protocol specifier, such as `https://`, `http://` and `ftp://`. Following is an example of pulling an image from a third party repository hub:

```
$ sudo docker pull registry.example.com/myapp
```

Searching Docker images

As we discussed in the previous section, the Docker Hub repository typically hosts both the official images as well as the images that have been contributed by the third-party Docker enthusiasts. At the time of writing this book, more than 14,000 images (also called the Dockerized application) were available for the users. These images can be used either as is, or as a building block for the user-specific applications.

You can search for the Docker images in the Docker Hub Registry by using the
`docker search` subcommand, as shown in this example:

```
$ sudo docker search mysql
```

The search on `mysql` will list 400 odd images, as follows:

NAME	DESCRIPTION	STARS	OFFICIAL	AUTOMATED
mysql	MySQL is the...	147	[OK]	
tutum/mysql	MySQL Server..	60		[OK]
orchardup/mysql		34		[OK]

`. . . OUTPUT TRUNCATED . . .`

As you can see in the preceding search output excerpts, the images are ordered
based on their star rating. The search result also indicates whether or not the image
is official. In order to stay in focus, in this example, we will show only two images.
Here, you can see the official version of `mysql`, which pulls a `147` star rating image
as its first result. The second result shows that this version of the `mysql` image was
published by the user `tutum`. The Docker containers are fast becoming the standard
for the building blocks of the distributed applications. A dynamic repository of
the Docker images will be realized with the help of the enthusiastic contribution
of several community members across the globe. The Repository-based software
engineering will make it easier for users and programmers to quickly code and
assemble their projects. The official repositories can be freely downloaded from the
Docker Hub Registry, and these are curated images. They represent a community
effort that is focused on providing a great base of images for applications, so that the
developers and the system administrators can focus on building new features and
functionalities, while minimizing their repetitive work on commodity scaffolding
and plumbing.

Based on the search queries in the Docker Hub Registry and the discussions
with many of the developer community members, the Docker company, which
spearheaded the Docker movement so powerfully and passionately, came to the
conclusion that the developer community wanted pre-built stacks of their favorite
programming languages. Specifically, the developers wanted to get to work as
quickly as possible writing code without wasting time wrestling with environments,
scaffolding, and dependencies.

Working with an interactive container

In the first chapter, we ran our first Hello World! container to get a feel of how the containerization technology works. In this section, we are going to run a container in an interactive mode. The docker run subcommand takes an image as an input and launches it as a container. You have to pass the -t and -i flags to the docker run subcommand in order to make the container interactive. The -i flag is the key driver, which makes the container interactive by grabbing the standard input (STDIN) of the container. The -t flag allocates a pseudo-TTY or a pseudo terminal (terminal emulator) and then assigns that to the container.

In the following example, we are going to launch an interactive container by using the ubuntu:14.04 image and /bin/bash as the command:

```
$ sudo docker run -i -t ubuntu:14.04 /bin/bash
```

Since the ubuntu image has not been downloaded yet, if we use the docker pull subcommand, then we will get the following message and the run command will start pulling the ubuntu image automatically with the following message:

```
Unable to find image 'ubuntu:14.04' locally

Pulling repository ubuntu
```

As soon as the download is completed, the container will be launched along with the ubuntu:14.04 image. It will also launch a bash shell within the container, because we have specified /bin/bash as the command to be executed. This will land us in a bash prompt, as shown here:

```
root@742718c21816:/#
```

The preceding bash prompt will confirm that our container has been launched successfully, and it is ready to take our input. If you are wondering about the Hex number 742718c21816 in the prompt, then it is nothing but the hostname of the container. In the Docker parlance, the hostname is the same as the container ID.

Let's quickly run a few commands interactively, and then confirm that what we mentioned about the prompt is correct, as shown here:

```
root@742718c21816:/# hostname
742718c21816
root@742718c21816:/# id
uid=0(root) gid=0(root) groups=0(root)
root@742718c21816:/# echo $PS1
```

```
${debian_chroot:+($debian_chroot)}\u@\h:\w\$
root@742718c21816:/#
```

From the preceding three commands, it is quite evident that the prompt was composed by using the user ID, the hostname, and the current working directory.

Now, let's use one of the niche features of Docker for detaching it from the interactive container and then look at the details that Docker manages for this container. Yes, we can detach it from our container by using the *Ctrl + P* and *Ctrl + Q* escape sequence. This escape sequence will detach the TTY from the container and land us in the Docker host prompt $, however the container will continue to run. The docker ps subcommand will list all the running containers and their important properties, as shown here:

```
$ sudo docker ps
CONTAINER ID        IMAGE               COMMAND             CREATED
STATUS              PORTS               NAMES
742718c21816        ubuntu:14.04        "/bin/bash"           About a
minute ago    Up About a minute                     jolly_lovelace
```

The docker ps subcommand will list out the following details:

- CONTAINER ID: This shows the container ID associated with the container. The container ID is a 64 Hex digit long random number. By default, the docker ps subcommand will show only 12 Hex digits. You can display all the 64 digits by using the --no-trunc flag (for example: sudo docker ps --no-trunc).

- IMAGE: This shows the image from which the Docker container has been crafted.

- COMMAND: This shows you the command executed during the container launch.

- CREATED: This tells you when the container was created.

- STATUS: This tells you the current status of the container.

- PORTS: This tells you if any port has been assigned to the container.

- NAMES: The Docker engine auto-generates a random container name by concatenating an adjective and a noun. Either the container ID or its name can be used to take further action on the container. The container name can be manually configured by using the --name option in the docker run subcommand.

Having looked at the container status, let's attach it back to our container by using the docker attach subcommand as shown in the following example. We can either use the container ID or use its name. In this example, we have used the container name. If you don't see the prompt, then press the *Enter* key again:

```
$ sudo docker attach jolly_lovelace
root@742718c21816:/#
```

 The Docker allows attaching with a container any number of times, which proves to be very handy for screen sharing.

The docker attach subcommand takes us back to the container prompt. Let's experiment a little more with the interactive container that is up and running by using these commands:

```
root@742718c21816:/# pwd
/
root@742718c21816:/# ls
bin    dev  home  lib64  mnt  proc  run   srv  tmp  var
boot   etc  lib   media  opt  root  sbin  sys  usr
root@742718c21816:/# cd usr
root@742718c21816:/usr# ls
bin  games  include  lib  local  sbin  share  src
root@742718c21816:/usr# exit
exit
$
```

As soon as the bash exit command is issued to the interactive container, it will terminate the bash shell process, which in turn will stop the container. As a result, we will land on the Docker Host's prompt $.

Tracking changes inside containers

In the previous section, we demonstrated how to craft a container taking ubuntu as a base image, and then running some basic commands, such as detaching and attaching the containers. In that process, we also exposed you to the docker ps subcommand, which provides the basic container management functionality. In this section, we will demonstrate how we can effectively track the changes that we introduced in our container and compare it with the image from which we launched the container.

Let's launch a container in the interactive mode, as we had done in the previous section:

```
$ sudo docker run -i -t ubuntu:14.04 /bin/bash
```

Let's change the directory to /home, as shown here:

```
root@d5ad60f174d3:/# cd /home
```

Now we can create three empty files by using the touch command as shown in the following code snippet. The first ls -l command will show that there are no files in the directory and the second ls -l command will show that there are three empty files:

```
root@d5ad60f174d3:/home# ls -l
total 0
root@d5ad60f174d3:/home# touch {abc,cde,fgh}
root@d5ad60f174d3:/home# ls -l
total 0
-rw-r--r-- 1 root root 0 Sep 29 10:54 abc
-rw-r--r-- 1 root root 0 Sep 29 10:54 cde
-rw-r--r-- 1 root root 0 Sep 29 10:54 fgh
root@d5ad60f174d3:/home#
```

The Docker engine elegantly manages its filesystem and it allows us to inspect a container filesystem by using the docker diff subcommand. In order to inspect the container filesystem, we can either detach it from the container or use another terminal of our Docker host and then issue the docker diff subcommand. Since we know that any ubuntu container has its hostname, which is a part of its prompt, and it is also the container's ID, we can directly run the docker diff subcommand by using the container ID that is taken from the prompt, as shown here:

```
$ sudo docker diff d5ad60f174d3
```

In the given example, the docker diff subcommand will generate four lines, shown here:

```
C /home
A /home/abc
A /home/cde
A /home/fgh
```

The preceding output indicates that the /home directory has been modified, which has been denoted by C, and the /home/abc, /home/cde and the /home/fgh files have been added, and these are denoted by A. In addition, D denotes deletion. Since we have not deleted any files, it is not in our sample output.

Controlling Docker containers

So far, we have discussed a few practical examples for clearly articulating the nitty-gritty of the Docker containers. In this section, let us introduce a few basic as well as a few advanced command structures for meticulously illustrating how the Docker containers can be managed.

The Docker engine enables you to start, stop, and restart a container with a set of docker subcommands. Let's begin with the docker stop subcommand, which stops a running container. When a user issues this command, the Docker engine sends SIGTERM (-15) to the main process, which is running inside the container. The **SIGTERM** signal requests the process to terminate itself gracefully. Most of the processes would handle this signal and facilitate a graceful exit. However, if this process fails to do so, then the Docker engine will wait for a grace period. Even after the grace period, if the process has not been terminated, then the Docker engine will forcefully terminate the process. The forceful termination is achieved by sending SIGKILL (-9). The **SIGKILL** signal cannot be caught or ignored, and so it will result in an abrupt termination of the process without a proper clean-up.

Now, let's launch our container and experiment with the docker stop subcommand, as shown here:

```
$ sudo docker run -i -t ubuntu:14.04 /bin/bash
root@da1c0f7daa2a:/#
```

Having launched the container, let's run the docker stop subcommand on this container by using the container ID that was taken from the prompt. Of course, we have to use a second screen or terminal to run this command, and the command will always echo back to the container ID, as shown here:

```
$ sudo docker stop da1c0f7daa2a
da1c0f7daa2a
```

Now, if we switch to the screen or terminal, where we were running the container, we will notice that the container is being terminated. If you observe a little more closely, you will also notice the text `exit` next to the container prompt. This has happened due to the SIGTERM handling mechanism of the bash shell, as shown here:

```
root@da1c0f7daa2a:/# exit
$
```

If we take it one step further and run the `docker ps` subcommand, then we will not find this container anywhere in the list. The fact is that the `docker ps` subcommand, by default, always lists the container that is in the running state. Since our container is in the stopped state, it has been comfortably left out of the list. Now, you might ask, how do we see the container that is in the stopped state? Well, the `docker ps` subcommand takes an additional argument `-a`, which will list all the containers in that Docker host irrespective of its status. This can be done by running the following command:

```
$ sudo docker ps -a
CONTAINER ID         IMAGE              COMMAND          PORTS
CREATED              STATUS                      PORTS
NAMES
da1c0f7daa2a         ubuntu:14.04        "/bin/bash"          20
minutes ago          Exited (0) 10 minutes ago
desperate_engelbart
$
```

Next, let's look at the `docker start` subcommand, which is used for starting one or more stopped containers. A container could be moved to the stopped state either by the `docker stop` subcommand or by terminating the main process in the container either normally or abnormally. On a running container, this subcommand has no effect.

Let's `start` the previously stopped container by using the `docker start` subcommand, as follows:

```
$ sudo docker start da1c0f7daa2a
da1c0f7daa2a
$
```

By default, the `docker start` subcommand will not attach to the container. You can attach it to the container either by using the `-a` option in the `docker start` subcommand or by explicitly using the `docker attach` subcommand, as shown here:

```
$ sudo docker attach da1c0f7daa2a
root@da1c0f7daa2a:/#
```

Now let's run the `docker ps` and verify the container's running status, as shown here:

```
$ sudo docker ps
CONTAINER ID          IMAGE             COMMAND
CREATED               STATUS                        PORTS
NAMES

da1c0f7daa2a          ubuntu:14.04        "/bin/bash"            25
minutes ago           Up 3 minutes
desperate_engelbart
$
```

The `restart` command is a combination of the `stop` and the `start` functionality. In other words, the `restart` command will `stop` a running container by following the precise steps followed by the `docker stop` subcommand and then it will initiate the `start` process. This functionality will be executed by default through the `docker restart` subcommand.

The next important set of container-controlling subcommands are `docker pause` and `docker unpause`. The `docker pause` subcommands will essentially freeze the execution of all the processes within that container. Conversely, the `docker unpause` subcommand will unfreeze the execution of all the processes within that container and resume the execution from the point where it was frozen.

Having seen the technical explanation of `pause and unpause`, let's see a detailed example for illustrating how this feature works. We have used two screen or terminal scenarios. On one terminal, we have launched our container and used an infinite while loop for displaying the date and time, sleeping for 5 seconds, and then continuing the loop. We will run the following commands:

```
$ sudo docker run -i -t ubuntu:14.04 /bin/bash
root@c439077aa80a:/# while true; do date; sleep 5; done
Thu Oct  2 03:11:19 UTC 2014
Thu Oct  2 03:11:24 UTC 2014
```

```
Thu Oct   2 03:11:29 UTC 2014
Thu Oct   2 03:11:34 UTC 2014
Thu Oct   2 03:11:59 UTC 2014
Thu Oct   2 03:12:04 UTC 2014
Thu Oct   2 03:12:09 UTC 2014
Thu Oct   2 03:12:14 UTC 2014
Thu Oct   2 03:12:19 UTC 2014
Thu Oct   2 03:12:24 UTC 2014
Thu Oct   2 03:12:29 UTC 2014
Thu Oct   2 03:12:34 UTC 2014
$
```

Our little script has very faithfully printed the date and time every 5 seconds with an exception at the following position:

```
Thu Oct   2 03:11:34 UTC 2014
Thu Oct   2 03:11:59 UTC 2014
```

Here, we encountered a delay of 25 seconds, because this is when we initiated the docker pause subcommand on our container on the second terminal screen, as shown here:

```
$ sudo docker pause c439077aa80a
c439077aa80a
```

When we paused our container, we looked at the process status by using the docker ps subcommand on our container, which was on the same screen, and it clearly indicated that the container had been paused, as shown in this command result:

```
$ sudo docker ps
CONTAINER ID            IMAGE               COMMAND             CREATED
STATUS                  PORTS               NAMES
c439077aa80a            ubuntu:14.04        "/bin/bash"         47
seconds ago       Up 46 seconds (Paused)
ecstatic_torvalds
```

We continued on to issuing the docker unpause subcommand, which unfroze our container, continued its execution, and then started printing the date and time, as we saw in the preceding command, shown here:

```
$ sudo docker unpause c439077aa80a
c439077aa80a
```

We explained the pause and the unpause commands at the beginning of this section. Lastly, the container and the script running within it had been stopped by using the docker stop subcommand, as shown here:

```
$ sudo docker stop c439077aa80a
c439077aa80a
```

Housekeeping containers

In many of the previous examples, when we issued docker ps -a we saw the many stopped containers. These containers could continue to stay in the stopped status for ages, if we chose not to intervene. At the outset, it may look like a glitch, but in reality, we can perform operations, such as committing an image from a container, restarting the stopped container, and so on. However, not all the stopped containers will be reused, and each of these unused containers will take up the disk space in the filesystem of the Docker host. The Docker engine provides a couple of ways to alleviate this issue. Let's start exploring them.

During a container startup, we can instruct the Docker engine to clean up the container as soon as it reaches the stopped state. For this purpose, the docker run subcommand supports an --rm option (for example: sudo docker run -i -t --rm ubuntu:14.04 /bin/bash).

The other alternative is to list all the containers by using the -a option of the docker ps subcommand and then manually remove them by using the docker rm subcommand, as shown here:

```
$ sudo docker ps -a
CONTAINER ID IMAGE          COMMAND       CREATED       STATUS
                     PORTS    NAMES
7473f2568add ubuntu:14.04 "/bin/bash" 5 seconds ago Exited
  (0) 3 seconds ago       jolly_wilson
$ sudo docker rm 7473f2568add
7473f2568add
$
```

Two docker subcommands, that is, docker rm and docker ps, could be combined to automatically delete all the containers that are not currently running, as shown in the following command:

```
$ sudo docker rm 'sudo docker ps -aq --no-trunc'
```

In the preceding command, the command inside the back quotes will produce a list of the full container IDs of every container, running or otherwise, which will become the argument for the docker rm subcommand. Unless forced with the -f option to do otherwise, the docker rm subcommand will only remove the container that is not in the running state. It will generate the following error for the running container and then continue to the next container on the list:

```
Error response from daemon: You cannot remove a running container.
Stop the container before attempting removal or use -f
```

Building images from containers

So far, we have crafted a handful of containers by using the standard base images busybox and ubuntu. In this section, let us see how we can add more software to our base image on a running container and then convert that container into an image for future use.

Let's take ubuntu:14.04 as our base image, install the wget application, and then convert the running container to an image by performing the following steps:

1. Launch an ubuntu:14.04 container by using the docker run subcommand, shown here:

   ```
   $ sudo docker run -i -t ubuntu:14.04 /bin/bash
   ```

2. Having launched the container, let's quickly verify if wget is available for our image or not. We have used the which command with wget as an argument for this purpose and, in our case, it returns empty, which essentially means that it could not find any wget installation in this container. This command is run as follows:

   ```
   root@472c96295678:/# which wget
   root@472c96295678:/#
   ```

3. Now let's move on to the next step which involves the wget installation. Since it is a brand new ubuntu container, before installing wget, we must synchronize with the ubuntu package repository, as shown here:

   ```
   root@472c96295678:/# apt-get update
   ```

4. Once the ubuntu package repository synchronization is over, we can proceed toward installing wget, as shown here:

   ```
   root@472c96295678:/# apt-get install -y wget
   ```

5. Having completed the wget installation, let's confirm our installation of wget by invoking the which command with wget as an argument, as shown here:

```
root@472c96295678:/#which wget
/usr/bin/wget
root@472c96295678:/#
```

6. Installation of any software would alter the base image composition, which we can also trace by using the docker diff subcommand introduced in *Tracking changes inside containers* section of this chapter. From a second terminal or screen, we can issue the docker diff subcommand, as follows:

```
$ sudo docker diff 472c96295678
```

The preceding command would show a few hundred lines of modification to the ubuntu image. This modification includes the update on package repository, wget binary, and the support files for wget.

7. Finally, let's move to the most important step of committing the image. The Docker commit subcommand can be performed on a running or a stopped container. When commit is performed on a running container, the Docker engine will pause the container during the commit operation in order to avoid any data inconsistency. We strongly recommend performing the commit operation on a stopped container. We can commit a container to an image by the docker commit subcommand, as shown here:

```
$ sudo docker commit 472c96295678 \
               learningdocker/ubuntu_wget
a530f0a0238654fa741813fac39bba2cc14457aee079a7ae1fe1c64dc7e1ac
25
```

We have committed our image by using the name learningdocker/ubuntu_wget.

Step by step, we saw how to create an image from a container. Now, let's quickly list the images of our Docker host and see if this newly created image is a part of the image list by using the following command:

```
$ sudo docker images
REPOSITORY                      TAG              IMAGE ID
CREATED            VIRTUAL SIZE
learningdocker/ubuntu_wget    latest             a530f0a02386
48 seconds ago       221.3 MB
```

busybox		buildroot-2014.02	e72ac664f4f0
2 days ago	2.433 MB		
ubuntu		14.04	6b4e8a7373fe
2 days ago	194.8 MB		

From the preceding `docker images` subcommand output, it is quite evident that our image creation from the container has been quite successful.

Now that you have learned how to create an image from the containers by using a few easy steps, we would encourage you to predominantly use this method for testing purposes. The most elegant and the most recommended way of creating an image is to use the `Dockerfile` method, which will be introduced in the next chapter.

Launching a container as a daemon

We have already experimented with an interactive container, tracked the changes that were made to the containers, created images from the containers and then gained insights in the containerization paradigm. Now, let's move on to understanding the real workhorse of the Docker technology. Yes that's right. In this section, we will walk you through the steps that are required for launching a container in the detached mode; in other words, we will learn about the steps that are required for launching a container as a daemon. We will also view the text that is generated in the container.

The `docker run` subcommand supports an option -d, which will launch a container in a detached mode, that is, it will launch a container as a daemon. For the purpose of illustration, let's resort to our date and time script, which we used in the `pause` and `unpause` container example, as shown here:

```
$ sudo docker run -d ubuntu \
        /bin/bash -c "while true; do date; sleep 5; done"
0137d98ee363b44f22a48246ac5d460c65b67e4d7955aab6cbb0379ac421269b
```

The `docker logs` subcommand is used for viewing the output generated by our daemon container, as shown here:

```
$ sudo docker logs \
0137d98ee363b44f22a48246ac5d460c65b67e4d7955aab6cbb0379ac421269b
Sat Oct  4 17:41:04 UTC 2014
Sat Oct  4 17:41:09 UTC 2014
Sat Oct  4 17:41:14 UTC 2014
Sat Oct  4 17:41:19 UTC 2014
```

Summary

In this chapter, we described the knowledge that is gained in the post-implementation phases, primarily regarding the operational aspect of the Docker containers. We started the chapter by clarifying important terms, such as images, containers, registry, and repository, in order to enable you to acquire an unambiguous understanding of the concepts illustrated thereafter. We explained how to search for the images in the Docker repository. We also discussed the operation and handling of the Docker containers, how to track the changes inside the containers, how to control and housekeep the containers. In an easy-to-grasp manner, we will explain the process of the Docker image building in the next chapter.

3

Building Images

In the previous chapter, we explained the image and container handling, and its housekeeping techniques and tips to you in detail. In addition to that, we also have explained the standard procedure for installing any software package on a Docker container and then converting the container into an image for future usage and maneuvering. This chapter is quite different from the earlier ones, and it is in this chapter to clearly describe how the Docker images are built using `Dockerfile`, which is the standard way to bring forth the highly usable Docker images. Leveraging `Dockerfile` is the most competent way to build powerful images for the software development community.

We will cover the following topics in this chapter:

- Docker's integrated image building system
- Quick overview of the Dockerfile's syntax
- `Dockerfile` build instructions
- How Docker stores images

Docker's integrated image building system

The Docker images are the fundamental building blocks of containers. These images could be very basic operating environments, such as `busybox` or `ubuntu`, as we found while experimenting with Docker in the previous chapters. Alternatively, the images could craft advanced application stacks for the enterprise and cloud IT environments. As we discussed in the previous chapter, we could craft an image manually by launching a container from a base image, install all the required applications, make the necessary configuration file changes, and then commit the container as an image.

As a better alternative, we could resort to the automated approach of crafting the images by using `Dockerfile`. `Dockerfile` is a text-based build script that contains special instructions in a sequence for building the right and relevant images from the base images. The sequential instructions inside the `Dockerfile` can include the base image selection, installing the required application, adding the configuration and the data files, and automatically running the services as well as exposing those services to the external world. Thus the Dockerfile-based automated build system has simplified the image-building process. It also offers a great deal of flexibility in the way in which the build instructions are organized and in the way in which they visualize the complete build process.

The Docker engine tightly integrates this build process with the help of the `docker build` subcommand. In the client-server paradigm of Docker, the Docker server (or daemon) is responsible for the complete build process and the Docker command line interface is responsible for transferring the build context, including transferring `Dockerfile` to the daemon.

In order to have a sneak peak into the `Dockerfile` integrated build system in this section, we will introduce you to a basic `Dockerfile`. Then we will explain the steps for converting that `Dockerfile` into an image, and then launching a container from that image. Our `Dockerfile` is made up of two instructions, as shown here:

```
$ cat Dockerfile
FROM busybox:latest
CMD echo Hello World!!
```

In the following, we will discuss the two instructions mentioned earlier:

- The first instruction is for choosing the base image selection. In this example, we will select the `busybox:latest` image

- The second instruction is for carrying out the command CMD, which instructs the container to `echo Hello World!!`.

Now, let's proceed towards generating a Docker image by using the preceding `Dockerfile` by calling `docker build` along with the path of `Dockerfile`. In our example, we will invoke the `docker build` subcommand from the directory where we have stored `Dockerfile`, and the path will be specified by the following command:

```
$ sudo docker build .
```

After issuing the preceding command, the `build` process will begin by sending `build context` to the `daemon` and then display the text shown here:

```
Sending build context to Docker daemon 3.072 kB
Sending build context to Docker daemon
Step 0 : from busybox:latest
```

The build process would continue and, after completing itself, it will display the following:

```
Successfully built 0a2abe57c325
```

In the preceding example, the image was built by the IMAGE ID 0a2abe57c325. Let's use this image to launch a container by using the `docker run` subcommand as follows:

```
$ sudo docker run 0a2abe57c325
Hello World!!
```

Cool, isn't it? With very little effort, we have been able to craft an image with `busybox` as the base image, and we have been able to extend that image to produce `Hello World!!`. This is a simple application, but the enterprise-scale images can also be realized by using the same technology.

Now let's look at the image details by using the `docker images` subcommand, as shown here:

```
$ sudo docker images
REPOSITORY      TAG         IMAGE ID       CREATED        VIRTUAL SIZE
<none>          <none>      0a2abe57c325   2 hours ago    2.433 MB
```

Here, you may be surprised to see that the IMAGE (REPOSITORY) and TAG name have been listed as <none>. This is because we did not specify any image or any TAG name when we built this image. You could specify an IMAGE name and optionally a TAG name by using the `docker tag` subcommand, as shown here:

```
$ sudo docker tag 0a2abe57c325 busyboxplus
```

The alternative approach is to build the image with an image name during the `build` time by using the `-t` option for the `docker build` subcommand, as shown here:

```
$ sudo docker build -t busyboxplus .
```

Since there is no change in the instructions in Dockerfile, the Docker engine will efficiently reuse the old image that has ID 0a2abe57c325 and update the image name to busyboxplus. By default, the build system would apply latest as the TAG name. This behavior can be modified by specifying the TAG name after the IMAGE name by having a : separator placed between them. That is, <image name>:<tag name> is the correct syntax for modifying behaviors, where <image name> is the name of the image and <tag name> is the name of the tag.

Once again, let's look at the image details by using the docker images subcommand, and you will notice that the image (Repository) name is busyboxplus and the tag name is latest:

```
$ sudo docker images
REPOSITORY       TAG           IMAGE ID        CREATED         VIRTUAL SIZE
busyboxplus      latest        0a2abe57c325    2 hours ago     2.433 MB
```

Building images with an image name is always recommended as the best practice.

Having experienced the magic of Dockerfile, in the subsequent sections we will introduce you to the syntax or the format of Dockerfile and explain a dozen Dockerfile instructions.

 The latest Docker release (1.5) has incorporated an additional option (-f) in the docker build subcommand, and it is used for specifying a Dockerfile with an alternative name.

A quick overview of the Dockerfile's syntax

In this section, we will explain the syntax or the format of Dockerfile. A Dockerfile is made up of instructions, comments, and empty lines, as shown here:

```
# Comment

INSTRUCTION arguments
```

The instruction line of `Dockerfile` is made up of two components, where the instruction line begins with the instruction itself, which is followed by the arguments for the instruction. The instruction could be written in any case, in other words, it is case-insensitive. However, the standard practice or convention is to use *uppercase* in order to differentiate it from the arguments. Let's take another look at the content of `Dockerfile` in our previous example:

```
FROM busybox:latest
CMD echo Hello World!!
```

Here, `FROM` is an instruction which has taken `busybox:latest` as an argument, and `CMD` is an instruction which has taken `echo Hello World!!` as an argument.

The comment line in `Dockerfile` must begin with the # symbol. The # symbol after an instruction is considered as an argument. If the # symbol is preceded by a whitespace, then the `docker build` system would consider that as an unknown instruction and skip the line. Now, let's better understand these mentioned cases with the help of an example to get a better understanding of the comment line:

- A valid `Dockerfile` comment line always begins with a # symbol as the first character of the line:

  ```
  # This is my first Dockerfile comment
  ```

- The # symbol can be a part of an argument:

  ```
  CMD echo ### Welcome to Docker ###
  ```

- If the # symbol is preceded by a whitespace, then it is considered as an unknown instruction by the build system:

  ```
  # this is an invalid comment line
  ```

The `docker build` system ignores any empty line in the `Dockerfile`, and so the author of `Dockerfile` is encouraged to add comments and empty lines to substantially improve the readability of `Dockerfile`.

The Dockerfile build instructions

So far, we have looked at the integrated build system, the `Dockerfile` syntax and a sample life cycle, including how a sample `Dockerfile` is leveraged to generate an image and how a container gets spun off from that image. In this section, we will introduce the `Dockerfile` instructions, their syntax, and a few fitting examples.

The FROM instruction

The FROM instruction is the most important one and it is the first valid instruction of a Dockerfile. It sets the base image for the build process. The subsequent instructions would use this base image and build on top of it. The docker build system lets you flexibly use the images built by anyone. You can also extend them by adding more precise and practical features to them. By default, the docker build system looks in the Docker host for the images. However, if the image is not found in the Docker host, then the docker build system will pull the image from the publicly available Docker Hub Registry. The docker build system will return an error if it can not find the specified image in the Docker host and the Docker Hub Registry.

The FROM instruction has the following syntax:

```
FROM <image>[:<tag>]
```

In the preceding code statement, note the following:

- <image>: This is the name of the image which will be used as the base image.
- <tag>: This is the optional tag qualifier for that image. If any tag qualifier has not been specified, then the tag latest is assumed.

Here is an example of the FROM instruction with the image name centos:

```
FROM centos
```

Here is another example of the FROM instruction with the image name ubuntu and the tag qualifier 14.04:

```
FROM ubuntu:14.04
```

Docker allows multiple FROM instructions in a single Dockerfile in order to create multiple images. The Docker build system will pull all the images specified in the FROM instruction. Docker does not provide any mechanism for naming the individual images that are generated with the help of multiple FROM instructions. We strongly discourage using multiple FROM instructions in a single Dockerfile, as damaging conflicts could arise.

The MAINTAINER instruction

The MAINTAINER instruction is an informational instruction of a Dockerfile. This instruction capability enables the authors to set the details in an image. Docker does not place any restrictions on placing the MAINTAINER instruction in Dockerfile. However, it is strongly recommended that you should place it after the FROM instruction.

The following is the syntax of the MAINTAINER instruction, where <author's detail> can be in any text. However, it is strongly recommended that you use the image author's name and the e-mail address, as shown in this code syntax:

```
MAINTAINER <author's detail>
```

Here is an example of the MAINTAINER instruction with the author name and the e-mail address:

```
MAINTAINER Dr. Peter <peterindia@gmail.com>
```

The COPY instruction

The COPY instruction enables you to copy the files from the Docker host to the filesystem of the new image. The following is the syntax of the COPY instruction:

```
COPY <src> ... <dst>
```

The preceding code terms bear the explanations shown here:

- <src>: This is the source directory, the file in the build context, or the directory from where the docker build subcommand was invoked.
- ...: This indicates that multiple source files can either be specified directly or be specified by wildcards.
- <dst>: This is the destination path for the new image into which the source file or directory will get copied. If multiple files have been specified, then the destination path must be a directory and it must end with a slash /.

Using an absolute path for the destination directory or a file is recommended. In the absence of an absolute path, the COPY instruction will assume that the destination path will start from root /. The COPY instruction is powerful enough for creating a new directory and for overwriting the filesystem in the newly created image.

In the following example, we will copy the html directory from the source build context to /var/www/html, which is in the image filesystem, by using the COPY instruction, as shown here:

```
COPY html /var/www/html
```

Here is another example of the multiple files (httpd.conf and magic) that will be copied from the source build context to /etc/httpd/conf/, which is in the image filesystem:

```
COPY httpd.conf magic /etc/httpd/conf/
```

The ADD instruction

The ADD instruction is similar to the COPY instruction. However, in addition to the functionality supported by the COPY instruction, the ADD instruction can handle the TAR files and the remote URLs. We can annotate the ADD instruction as COPY on steroids.

The following is the syntax of the ADD instruction:

```
ADD <src> ... <dst>
```

The arguments of the ADD instruction are very similar to those of the COPY instruction, as shown here:

- <src>: This is either the source directory or the file that is in the build context or in the directory from where the docker build subcommand will be invoked. However, the noteworthy difference is that the source can either be a TAR file stored in the build context or be a remote URL.

- ...: This indicates that the multiple source files can either be specified directly or be specified by using wildcards.

- <dst>: This is the destination path for the new image into which the source file or directory will be copied.

Here is an example for demonstrating the procedure for copying multiple source files to the various destination directories in the target image filesystem. In this example, we have taken a TAR file (web-page-config.tar) in the source build context with the http daemon configuration file and the files for the web pages are stored in the appropriate directory structure, as shown here:

```
$ tar tf web-page-config.tar
etc/httpd/conf/httpd.conf
var/www/html/index.html
var/www/html/aboutus.html
var/www/html/images/welcome.gif
var/www/html/images/banner.gif
```

The next line in the Dockerfile content has an ADD instruction for copying the TAR file (web-page-config.tar) to the target image and extracting the TAR file from the root directory (/) of the target image, as shown here:

```
ADD web-page-config.tar /
```

Thus the TAR option of the ADD instruction can be used for copying multiple files to the target image.

The ENV instruction

The ENV instruction sets an environment variable in the new image. An environment variable is a key-value pair, which can be accessed by any script or application. The Linux applications use the environment variables a lot for a starting configuration.

The following line forms the syntax of the ENV instruction:

```
ENV <key> <value>
```

Here, the code terms indicate the following:

- `<key>`: This is the environment variable
- `<value>`: This is the value that is to be set for the environment variable

The following lines give two examples for the ENV instruction, where in the first line DEBUG_LVL has been set to 3 and, in the second line, APACHE_LOG_DIR has been set to /var/log/apache:

```
ENV DEBUG_LVL 3
ENV APACHE_LOG_DIR /var/log/apache
```

The USER instruction

The USER instruction sets the start up user ID or user Name in the new image. By default, the containers will be launched with root as the user ID or UID. Essentially, the USER instruction will modify the default user ID from root to the one specified in this instruction.

The syntax of the USER instruction is as follows:

```
USER <UID>|<UName>
```

The USER instructions accept either `<UID>` or `<UName>` as its argument:

- `<UID>`: This is a numerical user ID
- `<UName>`: This is a valid user Name

The following is an example for setting the default user ID at the time of startup to 73. Here 73 is the numerical ID of the user:

```
USER 73
```

However, it is recommended that you have a valid user ID to match with the /etc/passwd file, the user ID can contain any random numerical value. However, the user Name must match with a valid user name in the /etc/passwd file, otherwise the docker run subcommand will fail and it will display the following error message:

```
finalize namespace setup user get supplementary groups Unable to find user
```

The WORKDIR instruction

The WORKDIR instruction changes the current working directory from / to the path specified by this instruction. The ensuing instructions, such as RUN, CMD, and ENTRYPOINT will also work on the directory set by the WORKDIR instruction.

The following line gives the appropriate syntax for the WORKDIR instruction:

```
WORKDIR <dirpath>
```

Here, <dirpath> is the path for the working directory to set in. The path can be either absolute or relative. In case of a relative path, it will be relative to the previous path set by the WORKDIR instruction. If the specified directory is not found in the target image filesystem, then the director will be created.

The following line is a clear example of the WORKDIR instruction in a Dockerfile:

```
WORKDIR /var/log
```

The VOLUME instruction

The VOLUME instruction creates a directory in the image filesystem, which can later be used for mounting volumes from the Docker host or the other containers.

The VOLUME instruction has two types of syntax, as shown here:

- The first type is either exec or JSON array (all values must be within double-quotes (")):

  ```
  VOLUME ["<mountpoint>"]
  ```

- The second type is shell, as shown here:

  ```
  VOLUME <mountpoint>
  ```

  In the preceding line, <mountpoint> is the mount point that has to be created in the new image.

The EXPOSE instruction

The EXPOSE instruction opens up a container network port for communicating between the container and the external world.

The syntax of the EXPOSE instruction is as follows:

```
EXPOSE <port>[/<proto>] [<port>[/<proto>]...]
```

Here, the code terms mean the following:

- <port>: This is the network port that has to be exposed to the outside world.
- <proto>: This is an optional field provided for a specific transport protocol, such as TCP and UDP. If no transport protocol has been specified, then TCP is assumed to be the transport protocol.

The EXPOSE instruction allows you to specify multiple ports in a single line.

The following is an example of the EXPOSE instruction inside a Dockerfile exposing the port number 7373 as a UDP port and the port number 8080 as a TCP port. As mentioned earlier, if the transport protocol has not been specified, then the TCP transport is assumed to be the transport protocol:

```
EXPOSE 7373/udp 8080
```

The RUN instruction

The RUN instruction is the real workhorse during the build time, and it can run any command. The general recommendation is to execute multiple commands by using one RUN instruction. This reduces the layers in the resulting Docker image because the Docker system inherently creates a layer for each time an instruction is called in Dockerfile.

The RUN instruction has two types of syntax:

- The first is the shell type, as shown here:

  ```
  RUN <command>
  ```

  Here, the <command> is the shell command that has to be executed during the build time. If this type of syntax is to be used, then the command is always executed by using /bin/sh -c.

- The second syntax type is either exec or the JSON array, as shown here:

  ```
  RUN ["<exec>", "<arg-1>", ..., "<arg-n>"]
  ```

  Within this, the code terms mean the following:

  ○ `<exec>`: This is the executable to run during the build time.

  ○ `<arg-1>, ..., <arg-n>`: These are the variables (zero or more) number of the arguments for the executable.

Unlike the first type of syntax, this type does not invoke /bin/sh -c. Therefore, the types of shell processing, such as the variable substitution ($USER) and the wild card substitution (*, ?), do not happen in this type. If shell processing is critical for you, then you are encouraged to use the shell type. However, if you still prefer the exec (JSON array type) type, then use your preferred shell as the executable and supply the command as an argument.

For example, RUN ["bash", "-c", "rm", "-rf", "/tmp/abc"].

Now let's look at a few examples of the RUN instruction. In the first example, we will use the RUN instruction for adding a greeting line to the .bashrc file in the target image filesystem, as shown here:

```
RUN echo "echo Welcome to Docker!" >> /root/.bashrc
```

The second example is a Dockerfile, which has the instructions for crafting an Apache2 application image on top of the Ubuntu 14.04 base image. The ensuing steps will explain the Dockerfile instructions line by line:

1. We are going to build an image by using ubuntu:14.04 as the base image using the FROM instruction, as shown here:

   ```
   ##########################################
   # Dockerfile to build an Apache2 image
   ##########################################
   # Base image is Ubuntu
   FROM ubuntu:14.04
   ```

2. Set the author's details by using the MAINTAINER instruction, as shown here:

   ```
   # Author: Dr. Peter
   MAINTAINER Dr. Peter <peterindia@gmail.com>
   ```

3. By using one RUN instruction, we will synchronize the apt repository source list, install the apache2 package, and then clean the retrieved files, as shown here:

```
# Install apache2 package
RUN apt-get update && \
    apt-get install -y apache2 && \
    apt-get clean
```

The CMD instruction

The CMD instruction can run any command (or application), which is similar to the RUN instruction. However, the major difference between those two is the time of execution. The command supplied through the RUN instruction is executed during the build time, whereas the command specified through the CMD instruction is executed when the container is launched from the newly created image. Therefore, the CMD instruction provides a default execution for this container. However, it can be overridden by the docker run subcommand arguments. When the application terminates, the container will also terminate along with the application and vice versa.

The CMD instruction has three types of syntax, as shown here:

- The first syntax type is the shell type, as shown here:
  ```
  CMD <command>
  ```

  Within this, the <command> is the shell command, which has to be executed during the launch of the container. If this type of syntax is used, then the command is always executed by using /bin/sh -c.

- The second type of syntax is exec or the JSON array, as shown here:
  ```
  CMD ["<exec>", "<arg-1>", ..., "<arg-n>"]
  ```

  Within this, the code terms mean the following:

  ○ <exec>: This is the executable, which is to be run during the container launch time.

  ○ <arg-1>, ..., <arg-n>: These are the variable (zero or more) numbers of the arguments for the executable.

- The third type of syntax is also exec or the JSON array, which is similar to the previous type. However, this type is used for setting the default parameters to the ENTRYPOINT instruction, as shown here:

```
CMD ["<arg-1>", ..., "<arg-n>"]
```

Within this, the code terms mean the following:

- ° <arg-1>, ..., <arg-n>: These are the variable (zero or more) numbers of the arguments for the ENTRYPOINT instruction, which will be explained in the next section.

Syntactically, you can add more than one CMD instruction in Dockerfile. However, the build system would ignore all the CMD instructions except for the last one. In other words, in the case of multiple CMD instructions, only the last CMD instruction would be effective.

Here, in this example, let's craft an image by using Dockerfile with the CMD instruction for providing a default execution, and then launching a container by using the crafted image. The following is Dockerfile with a CMD instruction to echo a text:

```
########################################################
# Dockerfile to demonstrate the behaviour of CMD
########################################################
# Build from base image busybox:latest
FROM busybox:latest
# Author: Dr. Peter
MAINTAINER Dr. Peter <peterindia@gmail.com>
# Set command for CMD
CMD ["echo", "Dockerfile CMD demo"]
```

Now, let's build a Docker image by using the docker build subcommand and cmd-demo as the image name. The docker build system will read the instruction from the Dockerfile, which is stored in the current directory (.), and craft the image accordingly as shown here:

```
$ sudo docker build -t cmd-demo .
```

Having built the image, we can launch the container by using the docker run subcommand, as shown here:

```
$ sudo docker run cmd-demo
Dockerfile CMD demo
```

Cool, isn't it? We have given a default execution for our container and our container has faithfully echoed `Dockerfile CMD demo`. However, this default execution can be easily overridden by passing another command as an argument to the `docker run` subcommand, as shown in the following example:

```
$ sudo docker run cmd-demo echo Override CMD demo
Override CMD demo
```

The ENTRYPOINT instruction

The `ENTRYPOINT` instruction will help in crafting an image for running an application (entry point) during the complete life cycle of the container, which would have been spun out of the image. When the entry point application is terminated, the container would also be terminated along with the application and vice versa. Therefore, the `ENTRYPOINT` instruction would make the container function like an executable. Functionally, `ENTRYPOINT` is akin to the `CMD` instruction, but the major difference between the two is that the entry point application is launched by using the `ENTRYPOINT` instruction, which cannot be overridden by using the `docker run` subcommand arguments. However, these `docker run` subcommand arguments will be passed as additional arguments to the entry point application. Having said this, Docker provides a mechanism for overriding the entry point application through the `--entrypoint` option in the `docker run` subcommand. The `--entrypoint` option can accept only word as its argument, and so it has limited functionality.

Syntactically, the `ENTRYPOINT` instruction is very similar to the `RUN` and `CMD` instructions, and it has two types of syntax, as shown here:

- The first type of syntax is the shell type, as shown here:

    ```
    ENTRYPOINT <command>
    ```

    Here, `<command>` is the shell command, which is executed during the launch of the container. If this type of syntax is used, then the command is always executed by using `/bin/sh -c`.

- The second type of syntax is exec or the JSON array, as shown here:

    ```
    ENTRYPOINT ["<exec>", "<arg-1>", ..., "<arg-n>"]
    ```

    Within this, the code terms mean the following:

    - `<exec>`: This is the executable, which has to be run during the container launch time.
    - `<arg-1>, ..., <arg-n>`: These are the variable (zero or more) numbers of arguments for the executable.

Syntactically, you can have more than one ENTRYPOINT instruction in a Dockerfile. However, the build system will ignore all the ENTRYPOINT instructions except the last one. In other words, in the case of multiple ENTRYPOINT instructions, only the last ENTRYPOINT instruction will be effective.

In order to gain a better understanding of the ENTRYPOINT instruction, let's craft an image by using Dockerfile with the ENTRYPOINT instruction, and then launching a container by using the crafted image. The following is Dockerfile with an ENTRYPOINT instruction to echo a text:

```
##########################################################
# Dockerfile to demonstrate the behaviour of ENTRYPOINT
##########################################################
# Build from base image busybox:latest
FROM busybox:latest
# Author: Dr. Peter
MAINTAINER Dr. Peter <peterindia@gmail.com>
# Set entrypoint command
ENTRYPOINT ["echo", "Dockerfile ENTRYPOINT demo"]
```

Now, let's build a Docker image by using the docker build as the subcommand and entrypoint-demo as the image name. The docker build system would read the instruction from Dockerfile stored in the current directory (.) and craft the image, as shown here:

```
$ sudo docker build -t entrypoint-demo .
```

Having built the image, we can launch the container by using the docker run subcommand:

```
$ sudo docker run entrypoint-demo
Dockerfile ENTRYPOINT demo
```

Here, the container will run like an executable by echoing the Dockerfile ENTRYPOINT demo string and then it will exit immediately. If we pass any additional arguments to the docker run subcommand, then the additional argument would be passed to the entry point command. The following is a demonstration of launching the same image with the additional arguments given to the docker run subcommand:

```
$ sudo docker run entrypoint-demo with additional arguments
Dockerfile ENTRYPOINT demo with additional arguments
```

Now, let's see an example where we override the build time entry point application with the `--entrypoint` option and then launch a shell (`/bin/sh`) in the `docker run` subcommand, as shown here:

```
$ sudo docker run --entrypoint="/bin/sh" entrypoint-demo
/ #
```

The ONBUILD instruction

The `ONBUILD` instruction registers a build instruction to an image and this is triggered when another image is built by using this image as its base image. Any build instruction can be registered as a trigger and those instructions will be triggered immediately after the `FROM` instruction in the downstream `Dockerfile`. Therefore, the `ONBUILD` instruction can be used to defer the execution of the build instruction from the base image to the target image.

The syntax of the `ONBUILD` instruction is as follows:

```
ONBUILD <INSTRUCTION>
```

Within this, `<INSTRUCTION>` is another `Dockerfile` build instruction, which will be triggered later. The `ONBUILD` instruction does not allow the chaining of another `ONBUILD` instruction. In addition, it does not allow the `FROM` and `MAINTAINER` instructions as `ONBUILD` triggers.

Here is an example of the `ONBUILD` instruction:

```
ONBUILD ADD config /etc/appconfig
```

The .dockerignore file

In the *Docker's integrated image building system* section, we learnt that the `docker build` process will send the complete build context to the daemon. In a practical environment, the `docker build` context will contain many other working files and directories, which would never be built into the image. Nevertheless, the `docker build` system would still send those files to the daemon. So, you may be wondering how you can optimize the build process by not sending these working files to the daemon. Well, the folks behind Docker too have thought about that and given a very simple solution: using a `.dockerignore` file.

The .dockerignore is a newline-separated TEXT file, wherein you can provide the files and the directories which are to be excluded from the build process. The exclusion list in the file can have both the fully specified file or directory name and the wild cards.

The following snippet is a sample .dockerignore file through which the build system has been instructed to exclude the .git directory and all the files that have the .tmp extension:

```
.git
*.tmp
```

A brief overview of the Docker image management

As we have seen in the previous chapter and this chapter, there are many ways of getting a handle on a Docker image. You could download a fully set up application stack from the public repository by using the docker pull subcommand. Otherwise you could craft your own application stack either manually by using the docker commit subcommand or automatically by using Dockerfile and the docker build subcommand combination.

The Docker images are being positioned as the key building-blocks of the containerized applications that, in turn, enable the realization of distributed applications, which will be deployed on the cloud servers. The Docker images are built in layers, that is, the images can be built on top of other images. The original image is called the parent image and the one that is generated is called the child image. The base image is a bundle, which comprises an application's common dependencies. Each change that is made to the original image is stored as a separate layer. Each time you commit to a Docker image, you will create a new layer on the Docker image, and each change that is made to the original image will be stored as a separate layer. As the reusability of the layers is facilitated, making new Docker images becomes simple and fast. You can create a new Docker image by changing a single line in Dockerfile and you do not need to rebuild the whole stack.

Now that we have learnt about the layers in the Docker image, you may be wondering how one could visualize these layers in a Docker image. Well, the docker history subcommand is an excellent and handy tool for visualizing the image layers.

Let's see a practical example to better understand the layering in the Docker images. For this purpose, let's follow these three steps:

1. Here, we have `Dockerfile` with the instructions for automatically building the Apache2 application image on top of the Ubuntu 14.04 base image. The RUN section of the previously crafted and used `Dockerfile` of this chapter will be reused in this section, as shown here:

    ```
    #############################################
    # Dockerfile to build an Apache2 image
    #############################################
    # Base image is Ubuntu
    FROM ubuntu:14.04
    # Author: Dr. Peter
    MAINTAINER Dr. Peter <peterindia@gmail.com>
    # Install apache2 package
    RUN apt-get update && \
        apt-get install -y apache2 && \
        apt-get clean
    ```

2. Now craft an image from the preceding `Dockerfile` by using the `docker build` subcommand, as shown here:

    ```
    $ sudo docker build -t apache2 .
    ```

3. Finally, let's visualize the layers in the Docker image by using the `docker history` subcommand:

    ```
    $ sudo docker history apache2
    ```

4. This will produce a detailed report on each layer of the `apache2` Docker image, as shown here:

    ```
    IMAGE            CREATED         CREATED BY                        SIZE
    aa83b67feeba     2 minutes ago   /bin/sh -c apt-get update &&
    apt-get inst   35.19 MB
    c7877665c770     3 minutes ago   /bin/sh -c #(nop) MAINTAINER
    Dr. Peter <peter   0 B
    9cbaf023786c     6 days ago      /bin/sh -c #(nop) CMD
    [/bin/bash]         0 B
    03db2b23cf03     6 days ago      /bin/sh -c apt-get update &&
    apt-get dist-upg   0 B
    8f321fc43180     6 days ago      /bin/sh -c sed -i
    's/^#\s*\(deb.*universe\)$/   1.895 kB
    ```

```
6a459d727ebb     6 days ago        /bin/sh -c rm -rf
/var/lib/apt/lists/*      0 B

2dcbbf65536c     6 days ago        /bin/sh -c echo '#!/bin/sh' >
/usr/sbin/polic 194.5 kB

97fd97495e49     6 days ago        /bin/sh -c #(nop) ADD
file:84c5e0e741a0235ef8  192.6 MB

511136ea3c5a     16 months ago                        0 B
```

Here, the `apache2` image is made up of ten image layers. The top two layers, the layers with image IDs `aa83b67feeba` and `c7877665c770`, are the result of `RUN` and `MAINTAINER` instructions in our `Dockerfile`. The remaining eight layers of the image will be pulled from the repository by the `FROM` instruction in our `Dockerfile`.

Best practices for writing Dockerfiles

It is an undisputable truth that a set of best practices always plays an indispensable role in elevating any new technology. There is a well-written document listing all the best practices for crafting a `Dockerfile`. We found it incredible, and so, we wanted to share it for your benefit. You can find it at `https://docs.docker.com/articles/dockerfile_best-practices/`.

Summary

Building the Docker images is a critical aspect of the Docker technology for streamlining the arduous task of containerization. As indicated before, the Docker initiative has turned out to be disruptive and transformative for the containerization paradigm. Dockerfile is the most prominent way for producing the competent Docker images, which can be used meticulously. We have illustrated all the commands, their syntax, and their usage techniques in order to empower you with all the easy-to-grasp details, and this will simplify the image-building process for you. We have supplied a bevy of examples in order to substantiate the inner meaning of each command. In the next chapter, we are going to discuss the Docker Hub, which is a well-designated store for storing and sharing the Docker images, and we will also discuss its profound contribution to the penetration of the containerization concept into the IT enterprises.

4
Publishing Images

In the previous chapter, we learned how to build Docker images. The next logical step is to publish these images in a public repository for public discovery and consumption. So, this chapter focuses on publishing images on the Docker Hub, and how to get the most out of the Docker Hub. We can create a new Docker image, using a `commit` command and a `Dockerfile`, build on it, and push it to the Docker Hub. The concept of a trusted repository will be discussed. This trusted repository is created from GitHub or Bitbucket. This can then be integrated with the Docker Hub to automatically build images, as a result of updates in the repository. This repository on GitHub is used to store the `Dockerfile`, which was previously created. Also, we will illustrate how worldwide organizations can enable their teams of developers to craft and contribute a variety of Docker images to be deposited in the Docker Hub. The Docker Hub REST APIs can be used for user management and manipulation of repository programmatically.

The following topics are covered in this chapter:

- Understanding the Docker Hub
- How to push images to the Docker Hub
- Automatic building of images
- Private repositories on the Docker Hub
- Creating organizations on the Docker Hub
- The Docker Hub REST API

Understanding the Docker Hub

The Docker Hub is a central place used for keeping the Docker images either in a public or private repository. The Docker Hub provides features, such as a repository for Docker images, user authentications, automated image builds, integration with GitHub or Bitbucket, and managing organizations and groups. The Docker Registry component of the Docker Hub manages the repository.

Docker Registry is a storage system used to store the images. Automated build is a feature of the Docker Hub, which is not open source yet, at the time of writing this book. The following diagram shows the typical features:

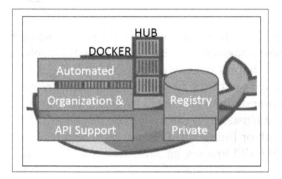

In order to work with the Docker Hub, you have to register with the Docker Hub, and create an account using the link at `https://hub.docker.com/account/signup`. You can update the **Username**, **Password**, and **Email Address**, as shown in the following screenshot:

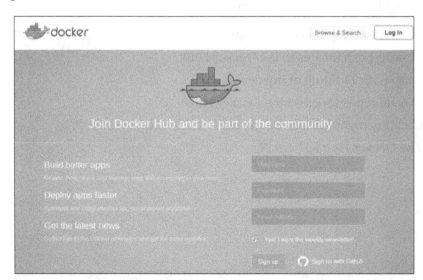

After completing the **Sign Up** process, you need to complete the verification received in an e-mail. After the e-mail verification is completed, you will see something similar to the following screenshot, when you login to the Docker Hub:

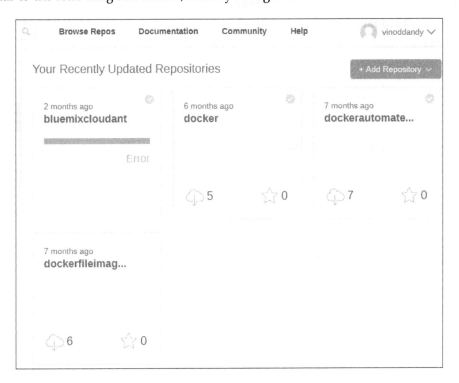

The creation of an account in the Docker Hub is completed successfully, and now you can log in to your Docker Hub account using `https://hub.docker.com/account/login/?next=/account/welcome/`, as shown in the following screenshot:

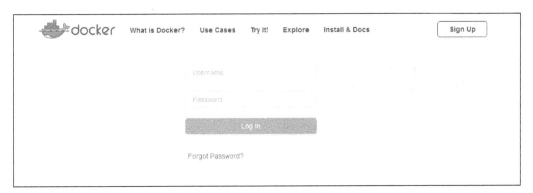

The Docker Hub also supports command-line access to the Docker Hub using a Ubuntu terminal:

```
ubuntu@ip-172-31-21-44:~$ sudo docker login
Username: vinoddandy
Password:
Email: vinoddandy@gmail.com
```

After a successful login, the output is as follows:

```
Login Succeeded
```

You can browse the available images in the Docker Hub, which are as follows:

Also, you can see your settings, update your profile, and get the details of the supported communities, such as Twitter, stackoverflow, #IRC, Google Groups, and GitHub.

Pushing images to the Docker Hub

Here, we will create a Docker image on the local machine, and push this image to the Docker Hub. You need to perform the following steps in this section:

1. Create a Docker image on the local machine by doing one of the following:
   - Using the `docker commit` sub command
   - Using the `docker commit` sub command with `Dockerfile`
2. Push this created image to the Docker Hub.
3. Delete the image from the Docker Hub.

We will use the Ubuntu base image, run the container, add a new directory and a new file, and then create a new image. In *Chapter 3, Building Images*, we have seen the creation of the Docker image using `Dockerfile`. You may refer to this to check for details of the `Dockerfile` syntax.

We will run the container with the name `containerforhub` from the base `ubuntu` image, as shown in the following terminal code:

```
$ sudo docker run -i --name="containerforhub" -t ubuntu /bin/bash
root@e3bb4b138daf:/#
```

Next, we'll create a new directory and file in the `containerforhub` container. We will also update the new file with some sample text to test later:

```
root@bd7cc5df6d96:/# mkdir mynewdir
root@bd7cc5df6d96:/# cd mynewdir
root@bd7cc5df6d96:/mynewdir# echo 'this is my new container to make image and then push to hub' >mynewfile
root@bd7cc5df6d96:/mynewdir# cat mynewfile
This is my new container to make image and then push to hub
root@bd7cc5df6d96:/mynewdir#
```

Let's build the new image with the `docker commit` command from the container, which has just been created. Note that the `commit` command would be executed from the host machine, from where the container is running, and not from inside this container:

```
$ sudo docker commit -m="NewImage" containerforhub
vinoddandy/imageforhub
3f10a35019234af2b39d5fab38566d586f00b565b99854544c4c698c4a395d03
```

Now, we have a new Docker image available on the local machine with the `vinoddandy/imageforhub` name. At this point in time, a new image with `mynewdir` and `mynewfile` is created locally.

We will log in to the Docker Hub using the `sudo docker login` command, as discussed earlier in this chapter.

Let's push this image to the Docker Hub from the host machine:

```
$ sudo docker push vinoddandy/imageforhub
The push refers to a repository [vinoddandy/imageforhub] (len: 1)
Sending image list
Pushing tag for rev [c664d94bbc55] on {https://cdn-registry-
1.docker.io/v1/repositories/vinoddandy/imageforhub/tags/latest
}
```

Now, we'll `login` to the Docker Hub and verify the image in **Repositories**.

To test the image from the Docker Hub, let's remove this image from the local machine. To remove the image, first we need to stop the container and then delete the container:

```
$ sudo docker stop containerforhub
$ sudo docker rm containerforhub
$
```

We will also delete the `vinoddandy/imageforhub` image:

```
$ sudo docker rmi vinoddandy/imageforhub
```

We will pull the newly created image from the Docker Hub, and run the new container on the local machine:

```
$ sudo docker run -i --name="newcontainerforhub" -t
vinoddandy/imageforhub /bin/bash
Unable to find image 'vinoddandy/imageforhub' locally
Pulling repository vinoddandy/imageforhub
c664d94bbc55: Pulling image (latest) from vinoddandy/imageforhub,
endpoint: http
c664d94bbc55: Download complete
5506de2b643b: Download complete
root@9bd40f1b5585:/# cat /mynewdir/mynewfile
This is my new container to make image and then push to hub
root@9bd40f1b5585:/#
```

So, we have pulled the latest image from the Docker Hub and created the container with the new image `vinoddandy/imageforhub`. Make a note that the `Unable to find image 'vinoddandy/imageforhub' locally` message confirms that the image is downloaded from the remote repository of the Docker Hub.

The text in `mynewfile` verifies that it is the same image, which was created earlier.

Finally, we will delete the image from the Docker Hub using `https://registry.hub.docker.com/u/vinoddandy/imageforhub/` and then click on **Delete Repository**, as shown in the following screenshot:

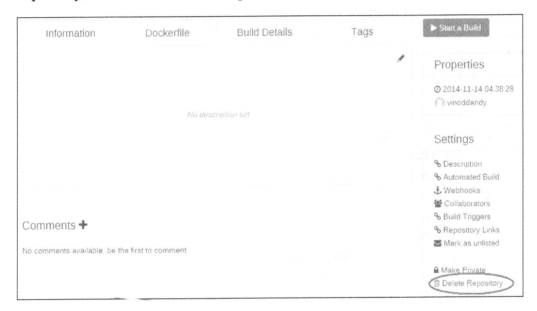

We'll again create this image but using the `Dockerfile` process. So, let's create the Docker image using the `Dockerfile` concept explained in *Chapter 3, Building Images*, and push this image to the Docker Hub.

The `Dockerfile` on the local machine is as follows:

```
##########################################
# Dockerfile to build a new image
##########################################
# Base image is Ubuntu
FROM ubuntu:14.04
# Author: Dr. Peter
```

```
MAINTAINER Dr. Peter <peterindia@gmail.com>
# create 'mynewdir' and 'mynewfile'
RUN mkdir mynewdir
RUN touch /mynewdir/mynewfile
# Write the message in file
RUN echo 'this is my new container to make image and then push to
hub' \
 >/mynewdir/mynewfile
```

Now we build the image locally using the following command:

```
$ sudo docker build -t="vinoddandy/dockerfileimageforhub" .
Sending build context to Docker daemon   2.56 kB
Sending build context to Docker daemon
Step 0 : FROM ubuntu:14.04
---> 5506de2b643b
Step 1 : MAINTAINER Vinod Singh <vinod.puchi@gmail.com>
---> Running in 9f6859e2ca75
---> a96cfbf4a810
removing intermediate container 9f6859e2ca75
Step 2 : RUN mkdir mynewdir
---> Running in d4eba2a31467
---> 14f4c15610a7
removing intermediate container d4eba2a31467
Step 3 : RUN touch /mynewdir/mynewfile
---> Running in 7d810a384819
---> b5bbd55f221c
removing intermediate container 7d810a384819
Step 4 : RUN echo 'this is my new container to make image and then
push to hub'
/mynewdir/mynewfile
---> Running in b7b48447e7b3
---> bcd8f63cfa79
removing intermediate container b7b48447e7b3
successfully built 224affbf9a65
ubuntu@ip-172-31-21-44:~/dockerfile_image_hub$
```

We'll run the container using this image, as shown here:

```
$ sudo docker run -i --name="dockerfilecontainerforhub" -t
vinoddandy/dockerfileimageforhub
root@d3130f21a408:/# cat /mynewdir/mynewfile
this is my new container to make image and then push to hub
```

This text in `mynewdir` confirms that the new image is built properly with a new directory and a new file.

Repeat the `login` process, in the Docker Hub, and push this newly created image:

```
$ sudo docker login
Username (vinoddandy):
Login Succeeded
$ sudo docker push vinoddandy/dockerfileimageforhub
The push refers to a repository [vinoddandy/dockerfileimageforhub]
(len: 1)
Sending image list
Pushing repository vinoddandy/dockerfileimageforhub (1 tags)
511136ea3c5a: Image already pushed, skipping
d497ad3926c8: Image already pushed, skipping
b5bbd55f221c: Image successfully pushed
bcd8f63cfa79: Image successfully pushed
224affbf9a65: Image successfully pushed
Pushing tag for rev [224affbf9a65] on
{https://cdn-registry-1.docker.io/v1/repos
itories/vinoddandy/dockerfileimageforhub/tags/latest}
$
```

Finally, we can verify the availability of the image on the Docker Hub:

Automating the building process for images

We learnt how to build images locally and push those images to the Docker Hub. The Docker Hub also has the capability to automatically build the image from `Dockerfile` kept in the repository of GitHub or Bitbucket. Automated builds are supported on both private and public repositories of GitHub and Bitbucket. The Docker Hub Registry keeps all the automated build images. The Docker Hub Registry is based on open source and can be accessed from `https://github.com/docker/docker-registry`.

We will discuss the steps needed to implement the automated build process:

1. We first connect the Docker Hub to my GitHub account.

   Login to the Docker Hub, and click on **View Profile** and then navigate to **Add Repository | Automated Build**, as shown in the following screenshot:

2. We now select **GitHub**:

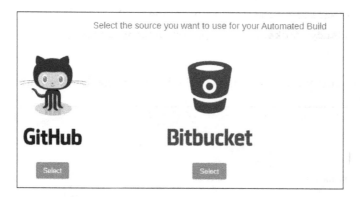

3. Once **GitHub** is selected, it will ask for authorization. Here, we will select **Public and Private**, as shown here:

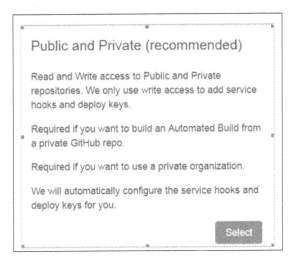

4. After clicking on **Select**, it will now show your GitHub repository:

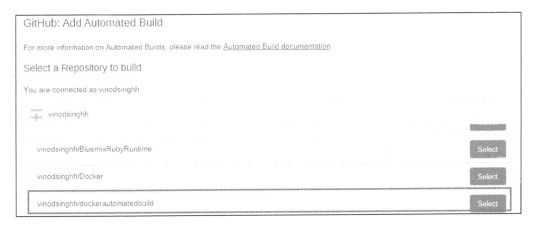

5. Click on the **Select** button of your repository **vinodsinghh/ dockerautomationbuild**, shown in the preceding screenshot:

6. We choose the default branch and update the tag with `Githubimage`. Also, we will keep the location as its default value, which is the root of our Docker Hub, as shown in the following screenshot:

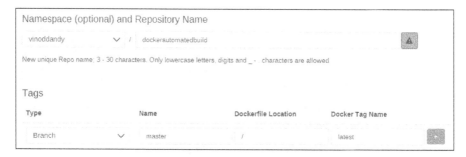

7. Finally, we will click on **Create Repository**, as shown in the preceding screenshot:

8. Click on **build details** to track your build status, as shown in the preceding screenshot. It will lead you to the following screenshot:

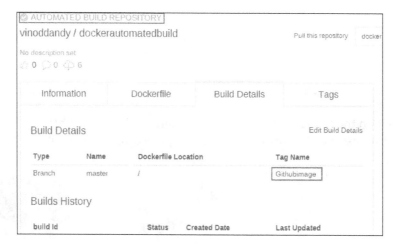

So, whenever the `Dockerfile` is updated in GitHub, the automated build gets triggered, and a new image will be stored in the Docker Hub Registry. We can always check the build history. We can change the `Dockerfile` on the local machine and push to GitHub. Then, we can see the automated build link of the Docker Hub at https://registry.hub.docker.com/u/vinoddandy/dockerautomatedbuild/builds_history/82194/.

Private repositories on the Docker Hub

The Docker Hub provides both a public and private repository. The public repository is free to users and private is a paid service. The plans with private repositories are available in different sizes, such as a micro, small, medium, or large subscription.

Docker has published their public repository code to open source at https://github.com/docker/docker-registry.

Normally, enterprises will not like to keep their Docker images either in a Docker public or private repository. They prefer to keep, maintain, and support their own repository. Hence, Docker also provides the option for enterprises to create and install their own repository.

Let's create a repository in the local machine using the registry image provided by Docker. We will run the registry container on the local machine, using the registry image from Docker:

```
$ sudo docker run -p 5000:5000 -d registry
768fb5bcbe3a5a774f4996f0758151b1e9917dec21aedf386c5742d44beafa41
```

In the automated build section, we built the `vinoddandy/dockerfileforhub` image. Let's tag the image ID `224affbf9a65` to our locally created `registry` image. This tagging of the image is needed for unique identification inside the local repository. This image `registry` may have multiple variants in the repository, so this `tag` will help you identify the particular image:

```
$ sudo docker tag
224affbf9a65localhost:5000/vinoddandy/dockerfileimageforhub
```

Once the tagging is done, push this image to a new registry using the `docker push` command:

```
$ sudo docker push localhost:5000/vinoddandy/dockerfile
imageforhub
```

```
The push refers to a repository
[localhost:5000/vinoddandy/dockerfileimageforhub
] (len: 1)
Sending image list
Pushing repository localhost:5000/vinoddandy/dockerfileimageforhub (1
tags)
511136ea3c5a: Image successfully pushed
d497ad3926c8: Image successfully pushed
------------------------------------------------------
224affbf9a65: Image successfully pushed
Pushing tag for rev [224affbf9a65] on
{http://localhost:5000/v1/repositories/vin
oddandy/dockerfileimageforhub/tags/latest}
ubuntu@ip-172-31-21-44:~$
```

Now, the new image is available in the local repository. You can now retrieve this image from the local registry and run the container. This task is left for you to complete.

Organizations and teams on the Docker Hub

One of the useful aspects of private repositories is that you can share them only with members of your organization or team. The Docker Hub lets you create organizations, where you can collaborate with your colleagues and manage private repositories. You can learn how to create and manage an organization.

The first step is to create an organization on the Docker Hub, as shown in the following screenshot:

Inside your organization, you can add more organizations, and then add members
to it:

The members of your organization and group can collaborate with the organization
and teams. This feature would be more useful in case of a private repository.

The REST APIs for the Docker Hub

The Docker Hub provides a REST API to integrate the Hub capabilities through
programs. The REST API is supported for both user as well as repository
management.

User management supports the following features:

- **User Login**: This is used for user login to the Docker Hub:

```
GET /v1/users
```

```
$ curl --raw -L --user vinoddandy:password
https://index.docker.io/v1/users
4
"OK"
0
$
```

- **User Register**: This is used for registration of a new user:

```
POST /v1/users
```

- **Update user**: This is used to update the user's password and e-mail:

```
PUT /v1/users/(usename)/
```

Repository management supports the following features:

- **Create a user repository**: This creates a user repository:

```
PUT /v1/repositories/(namespace)/(repo_name)/
```

```
$ curl --raw -L -X POST --post301 -H "Accept:application/json"
-H "Content-Type: application/json" --data-ascii '{"email":
"singh_vinod@yahoo.com", "password": "password", "username":
"singhvinod494" }' https://index.docker.io/v1/users
```

```
e
```

```
"User created"
```

```
0
```

After you create repositories, your repositories will be listed here, as shown in this screenshot:

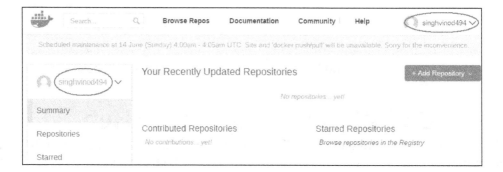

- **Delete a user repository**: This deletes a user repository:

```
DELETE /v1/repositories/(namespace)/(repo_name)/
```

- **Create a library repository**: This creates the library repository, and it is available only to Docker administrators:

```
PUT /v1/repositories/(repo_name)/
```

- **Delete a library repository**: This deletes the library repository, and it is available only to Docker administrators:

```
DELETE /v1/repositories/(repo_name)/
```

- **Update user repository images**: This updates the images of a user's repository:

```
PUT /v1/repositories/(namespace)/(repo_name)/images
```

- **List user repository images**: This lists the images of a user's repository:

  ```
  GET /v1/repositories/(namespace)/(repo_name)/images
  ```

- **Update library repository images**: This updates the images of a library repository:

  ```
  PUT /v1/repositories/(repo_name)/images
  ```

- **List library repository images**: This lists the images of a library repository:

  ```
  GET /v1/repositories/(repo_name)/images
  ```

- **Authorize a token for a library repository**: This authorizes a token for a library repository:

  ```
  PUT /v1/repositories/(repo_name)/auth
  ```

- **Authorize a token for a user repository**: This authorizes a token for a user's repository:

  ```
  PUT /v1/repositories/(namespace)/(repo_name)/auth
  ```

Summary

Docker images are the most prominent building blocks used for deriving real-world Docker containers that can be exposed as a service over any network. Developers can find and check images for their unique capabilities, and use them accordingly for their own purposes in bringing up highly usable, publicly discoverable, network-accessible, and cognitively composable containers. All the crafted images need to be put in a public registry repository. In this chapter, we clearly explained how to publish images in a repository. We also talked about the trusted repositories and their distinct characteristics. Finally, we demonstrated how the REST API for the repository can be leveraged to push in and play around with Docker images and user management programmatically.

The Docker images need to be stored in a public, controlled, and network-accessible location to be readily found and leveraged by worldwide software engineers and system administrators. The Docker Hub is being touted as the best-in-class method for centrally aggregating, curating, and managing Docker images, originating from Docker enthusiasts (internal as well as external). However, enterprises cannot afford to keep their Docker images in a public domain, and hence, the next chapter is dedicated to expose the steps needed for image deployment and management in private IT infrastructures.

5
Running Your Private Docker Infrastructure

In *Chapter 4, Publishing Images,* we discussed Docker images and clearly understood that Docker containers are the runtime implementations of Docker images. Docker images and containers are in plenty these days, as the containerization paradigm has taken the IT domain by storm. Therefore, there is a need for worldwide enterprises to keep their Docker images in their own private infrastructure for security considerations. So, the concept of deploying a Docker Hub to our own infrastructure has emerged and evolved. Docker Hubs are paramount and pertinent to register and then deposit the growing array of Docker images. Primarily, a Docker Hub is specially made to centralize and centrally manage information on:

- User accounts
- Checksums of the images
- Public namespaces

This chapter is developed with an a focus on providing all the relevant information to enable you and Docker container crafters to design, populate, and run their own private Docker Hubs in their own backyards. This chapter covers the following important topics:

- The Docker registry and index
- Docker registry use cases
- Run your own index and registry
- Push the image to a newly created registry

The Docker registry and index

Typically, a Docker Hub consists of a Docker index and registry. Docker clients can connect and interact with the Docker Hubs over a network. The registry has the following characteristics:

- It stores the images and graphs for a set of repositories
- It does not have user accounts data
- It has no notion of user accounts or authorization
- It delegates the authentication and authorization to the Docker Hub Authentication service
- It supports different storage backends (S3, cloud files, local filesystem, and so on)
- It doesn't have a local database
- It has a source code associated with it

The advanced features of the Docker registry include `bugsnag`, `new relic`, and `cors`. The `bugsnag` feature detects and diagnoses crashes in applications, `new relic` encapsulates the registry and monitors performance, and `cors` can be enabled to share resources outside our own registry domain. It is recommended that you deploy the registry to production environments using a proxy, such as nginx. You can also run the Docker registry directly on Ubuntu and Red Hat Linux-based systems.

Currently, the firm in charge of developing the Docker platform has released the Docker registry as an open source service on GitHub at `https://github.com/docker/docker-registry`. It is important to note that the Docker index is only a recommendation and nothing has been released by Docker as an open source project at the time of writing this book. In this chapter, we will start with a use case of the Docker registry, and then start with the actual deployment of the index elements and the Docker registry from GitHub.

Docker registry use cases

The following are the use cases of the Docker registry:

1. Pull or download an image
2. Push an image
3. Delete an image

We will now go through each of these use cases in detail:

1. **Pull or download an image**: The user requests an image using the Docker client from the index, the index, in turn responds back to the user with the registry details. Then, the Docker client will directly request the registry to get the required image. The registry authenticates the user with an index internally. As shown in the following diagram, image pulling is accomplished with the collaboration of the client, index, and registry modules:

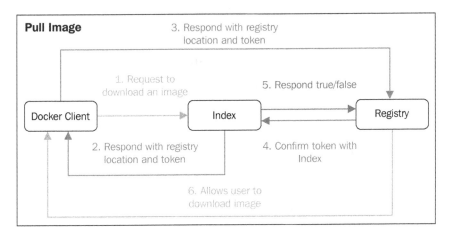

2. **Push an image**: A user requests to push the image, gets the registry information from the index, and then pushes the image directly to the registry. The registry authenticates the user with the index and, finally, responds to the user. The control flow is illustrated in the following diagram:

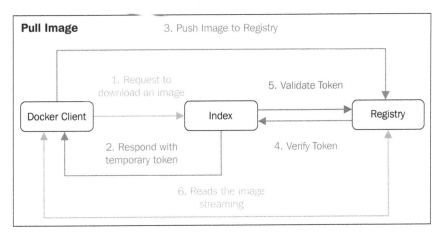

3. **Delete an image**: The user can also request to delete an image from the repository.

The user has the option to use the registry with or without the index. Use of the registry, without the index, is best suited for storing private images.

Run your own index and registry

In this section, we will perform the following steps to run our own index and registry, and finally, push the image:

1. Deployment of the index components and the registry from GitHub.
2. Configuration of nginx with the Docker Registry.
3. Set up SSL on the web server for secure communication.

Step 1 – Deployment of the index components and the registry from GitHub

The index components include `apache-utils` and `ngnix` for password authentication and the SSL feature for HTTPS support. The user must note that the current version of the Docker registry supports only HTTP to connect to the registry. So, it is mandatory for the user to deploy and use **Secure Sockets Layer (SSL)** to secure the data. SSL creates an encrypted connection between a web server and the client's web browser that allows private data to be transmitted without the issues of eavesdropping, data tampering, or message forgery. This is a proven way of securing the data using SSL certificates that is widely accepted.

The Docker registry is a Python application, and we can install Python on the local Ubuntu machine from `https://github.com/docker/docker-registry`, using the following command:

```
$ sudo apt-get -y install build-essential python-dev \
        libevent-dev python-pip liblzma-dev swig libssl-dev
```

Now, install the Docker registry:

```
$ sudo pip install docker-registry
```

This will update the Docker registry in the Python package and update the configuration file in the following path:

```
$ cd /usr/local/lib/python2.7/dist-
packages/config/
```

Copy the `config_sample.yml` file to `config.yml`:

```
$ sudo cp config_sample.yml config.yml
```

Docker, by default, saves its data in the `/tmp` directory, which can create problems because the `/tmp` folder is cleared on reboot on many Linux systems. Let's create a permanent folder to store our data:

```
$ sudo mkdir /var/docker-registry
```

Let's update our preceding `config.yml` file for this updated path for the following two locations. The updated code for the first location will look like this:

```
sqlalchemy_index_database:
    _env:SQLALCHEMY_INDEX_DATABASE:sqlite:////var/docker-
registry/docker-registry.db
```

The following is the code for the second location:

```
local: &local
    storage: local
    storage_path: _env:STORAGE_PATH:/var/docker-registry/registry
```

The other default configuration of the `config.yml` file works fine.

Now, let's start the Docker registry using `gunicorn`. Gunicorn, also known as Green Unicorn, is a Python **Web Server Gateway Interface (WSGI)** HTTP server for Linux systems:

```
$ sudo gunicorn --access-logfile - --debug -k gevent -b \
        0.0.0.0:5000 -w 1 docker_registry.wsgi:application
01/Dec/2014:04:59:23 +0000 WARNING: Cache storage disabled!
01/Dec/2014:04:59:23 +0000 WARNING: LRU cache disabled!
01/Dec/2014:04:59:23 +0000 DEBUG: Will return docker-
registry.drivers.file.Storage
```

Now, the Docker registry is up and running as a process on the user's local machine.

We can stop this process using *Ctrl + C*.

We can start a Linux service as follows:

1. Make a directory for the `docker-registry` tool:

   ```
   $ sudo mkdir -p /var/log/docker-registry
   ```

2. Create and update the file for the Docker registry configuration:

   ```
   $ sudo vi /etc/init/docker-registry.conf
   ```

3. Update the following content in the file:

```
description "Docker Registry"
start on runlevel [2345]
stop on runlevel [016]
respawn
respawn limit 10 5
script
exec gunicorn --access-logfile /var/log/docker-
registry/access.log --error-logfile /var/log/docker-
registry/server.log -k gevent --max-requests 100 --
graceful-timeout 3600 -t 3600 -b localhost:5000 -w 8
docker_registry.wsgi:application
end script
```

4. After saving the file, run the Docker registry service:

```
$ sudo service docker-registry start
docker-registry start/running, process 25760
```

5. Now secure this registry using `apache-utils`, by enabling the password protected feature, as shown here:

```
$ sudo apt-get -y install nginx apache2-utils
```

6. The user creates a login ID and password to access the Docker registry:

```
$ sudo htpasswd -c /etc/nginx/docker-registry.htpasswd vinod1
```

7. Enter the new password when prompted. At this point, we have the login ID and password to access the Docker registry.

Step 2 – Configuration of nginx with the Docker registry

Next, we need to tell nginx to use that authentication file (created in step 6 and step 7 of the previous section) to forward requests to our Docker registry.

We need to create the nginx configuration file. To do this, we need to follow these steps:

1. We create the ngnix configuration file by running the following command:

```
$ sudo vi /etc/nginx/sites-available/docker-registry
```

Update the file with the following content:

```
upstream docker-registry {
  server localhost:5000;
```

```
}
server {
 listen 8080;
 server_name my.docker.registry.com;
 # ssl on;
 # ssl_certificate /etc/ssl/certs/docker-registry;
 # ssl_certificate_key /etc/ssl/private/docker-registry;
 proxy_set_header Host          $http_host;    # required for
Docker client sake
 proxy_set_header X-Real-IP $remote_addr; # pass on real
client IP
 client_max_body_size 0; # disable any limits to avoid HTTP
413 for large image uploads
 # required to avoid HTTP 411: see Issue #1486
(https://github.com/dotcloud/docker/issues/1486)
 chunked_transfer_encoding on;
 location / {
     # let Nginx know about our auth file
     auth_basic              "Restricted";
     auth_basic_user_file    docker-registry.htpasswd;
     proxy_pass http://docker-registry;
 } location /_ping {
     auth_basic off;
     proxy_pass http://docker-registry;
 }   location /v1/_ping {
     auth_basic off;
     proxy_pass http://docker-registry;
 }
}
```

2. Make the soft link and restart the ngnix service:

```
$ sudo ln -s /etc/nginx/sites-available/docker-registry \
        /etc/nginx/sites-enabled/docker-registry
$ sudo service nginx restart
```

3. Let's check whether everything works fine. Run the following command, and we should get this output:

```
$ sudo curl localhost:5000
"\"docker-registry server\""
```

Great! So now we have the Docker registry running. Now, we have to check whether nginx worked as we expected it to. To do this, run the following command:

```
$ curl localhost:8080
```

This time, we will get an unauthorized message:

```
<html>
<head><title>401 Authorization Required</title></head>
<body bgcolor="white">
<center><h1>401 Authorization Required</h1></center>
<hr><center>nginx/1.4.6 (Ubuntu)</center>
</body>
</html>
```

Let's log in using the password created earlier:

```
$ curl vinod1:vinod1@localhost:8080
```

```
"\"docker-registry server\""ubuntu@ip-172-31-21-44:~$
```

This confirms that your Docker registry is password protected.

Step 3 – Set up SSL on the web server for secure communication

This is the final step to set up SSL on a local machine, which hosts the web server for the encryption of data. We create the following file:

```
$sudo vi /etc/nginx/sites-available/docker-registry
```

Update the file with the following content:

```
server {
 listen 8080;
 server_name mydomain.com;
 ssl on;
 ssl_certificate /etc/ssl/certs/docker-registry;
 ssl_certificate_key /etc/ssl/private/docker-registry;
```

Note that my Ubuntu machine is available on the Internet with the name mydomain.com and SSL is set up with the path for a certificate and key.

Let's sign the certificate as follows:

```
$ sudo mkdir ~/certs
$ sudo cd ~/certs
```

The root key is generated using `openssl`, using the following command:

```
$ sudo openssl genrsa -out devdockerCA.key 2048
Generating RSA private key, 2048 bit long modulus
..........+++
...................+++
e is 65537 (0x10001)
```

Now we have the root key, let's generate a root certificate (enter whatever you'd like to at the Command Prompt):

```
$ sudo openssl req -x509 -new -nodes -key devdockerCA.key -days  \
        10000 -out devdockerCA.crt
```

Then, generate a key for our server:

```
$ sudo openssl genrsa -out dev-docker-registry.com.key 2048
```

Now, we have to make a certificate signing request. Once we run the signing command, ensure that `Common Name` is our server name. This is mandatory and any deviation will result in an error:

```
$ sudo openssl req -new -key dev-docker-registry.com.key -out \
   dev-docker-registry.com.csr
```

Here, `Common Name` looks like `mydomain.com`. This is an Ubuntu VM running on AWS.

The output of the preceding command is shown as follows:

```
Country Name (2 letter code) [AU]:
State or Province Name (full name) [Some-State]:
Locality Name (eg, city) []:
Organization Name (eg, company) [Internet Widgits Pty Ltd]:
Organizational Unit Name (eg, section) []:
Common Name (e.g. server FQDN or YOUR name) []: mydomain.com
Email Address []:
Please enter the following 'extra' attributes
to be sent with your certificate request
A challenge password []:
An optional company name []:
```

The `challenge password` input is kept blank, and the user is also free to populate this. Then, we need to sign the certificate request, by running the following command:

```
$ sudo openssl x509 -req -in dev-docker-registry.com.csr -CA  \
    devdockerCA.crt -CAkey devdockerCA.key -CAcreateserial -out \
    dev-docker-registry.com.crt -days 10000
```

Now that we've generated all the files we need for our certificate to work, we need to copy these files to the correct places.

First, copy the certificate and key to the paths where nginx is expecting them to be:

```
$ sudo cp dev-docker-registry.com.crt /etc/ssl/certs/docker-registry
$ sudo chmod 777 /etc/ssl/certs/docker-registry
$ sudo cp dev-docker-registry.com.key /etc/ssl/private/docker-registry
$ sudo chmod 777 /etc/ssl/private/docker-registry
```

Note that we have created self-signed certificates, and they are signed by any known certificate authority, so we need to inform the registry that this is a legitimate certificate:

```
$ sudo mkdir /usr/local/share/ca-certificates/docker-dev-cert
```

```
$ sudo cp devdockerCA.crt /usr/local/share/ca-certificates/docker-dev-cert
```

```
$ sudo update-ca-certificates
```

```
Updating certificates in /etc/ssl/certs... 1 added, 0 removed; done.
```

```
Running hooks in /etc/ca-certificates/updated....done.
```

```
ubuntu@ip-172-31-21-44:~/certs$
```

Let's restart nginx to reload the configuration and SSL keys:

```
$ sudo service nginx restart
```

Now, we will test the SSL certificate to check whether it works fine. Since mydomain.com is not an Internet address, add the entry in /etc/hosts file:

```
172.31.24.44 mydomain.com
```

```
Now run the following command:
```
```
$ sudo curl https://vinod1:vinod1@ mydomain.com:8080
```
```
"\"docker-registry server\""ubuntu@ip-172-31-21-44:~$
```

So if all went well, you should see something like this:

```
"docker-registry server"
```

Push the image to the newly created Docker registry

Finally, push the image to the Docker registry. So, let's create an image on the local Ubuntu machine:

```
$ sudo docker run -t -i ubuntu /bin/bash
root@9593c56f9e70:/# echo "TEST" >/mydockerimage
root@9593c56f9e70:/# exit
$ sudo docker commit $(sudo docker ps -lq) vinod-image
e17b685ee6987bb0cd01b89d9edf81a9fc0a7ad565a7e85650c41fc7e5c0cf9e
```

Let's log in to the Docker registry created locally on the Ubuntu machine:

```
$ sudo docker --insecure-registry= mydomain.com:8080 \
    login https:// mydomain.com:8080
Username: vinod1
Password:
Email: vinod.puchi@gmail.com
Login Succeeded
```

Tag the image before pushing it to the registry:

```
$ sudo docker tag vinod-image mydomain.com:8080/vinod-image
```

Finally, use the push command to upload the image:

```
$ sudo docker push \
mydomain.com:8080/vinod-image
The push refers to a repository [mydomain.com
:8080/vinod-image] (len: 1)
Sending image list
Pushing repository mydomain.com:8080/vi
nod-image (1 tags)
511136ea3c5a: Image successfully pushed
5bc37dc2dfba: Image successfully pushed
-------------------------------------------------
e17b685ee698: Image successfully pushed
```

```
Pushing tag for rev [e17b685ee698] on {https:// mydomain.com
:8080/v1/repositories/vinod-image/tags/latest}
$
```

Now, remove the image from the local disk and `pull` it from the Docker registry:

```
$ sudo docker pull mydomain.com:8080/vinod-image
Pulling repository mydomain.com:8080/vi
nod-image
e17b685ee698: Pulling image (latest) from mydomain.com
17b685ee698: Download complete
dc07507cef42: Download complete
86ce37374f40: Download complete
Status: Downloaded newer image for mydomain.com:8080/vinod-image:latest
$
```

Summary

The Docker engine allows every value-adding software solution to be containerized, indexed, registered, and stocked. Docker is turning out to be a great tool for systematically developing, shipping, deploying, and running containers everywhere. While `docker.io` lets you upload your Docker creations to their registry for free, anything you upload there is publicly discoverable and accessible. Innovators and companies aren't keen on this and therefore, insist on for private Docker Hubs. In this chapter, we explained all the steps, syntaxes, and semantics for you in an easy-to-understand manner. We saw how to retrieve images to generate Docker containers and described how to push our images to the Docker registry in a secure manner in order to be found and used by authenticated developers. The authentication and authorization mechanisms, a major part of the whole process, have been explained in detail. Precisely speaking, this chapter is conceived and concretized as a guide for setting up your own Docker Hubs. As world organizations are showing exemplary interest in having containerized clouds, private container hubs are becoming more essential.

In the next chapter, we will dive deep into containers, which is the natural progression from images. We will demonstrate the capability to run services, such as a web server in a Docker container, and its interaction with the host machine and the outside world.

6
Running Services in a Container

We've reached so far, brick by brick, laying a strong and stimulating foundation on the fast-evolving Docker technology. We talked about the important building blocks of the highly usable and reusable Docker images. Further on, you can read the easy-to-employ techniques and tips on how to store and share Docker images through a well-designed storage framework. As usual, images will have to go through a series of verifications, validations, and refinements constantly in order to make them more right and relevant for the aspiring development community. In this chapter, we are going to take our learning to the next level by describing the steps towards creating a small web server, run the same inside a container, and connect to the web server from the external world.

In this chapter, we will cover the following topics:

- Container networking
- **Container as a Service (CaaS)** — building, running, exposing, and connecting to container services
- Publishing and retrieving container ports
- Binding a container to a specific IP address
- Auto-generating the Docker host port
- Port binding using the EXPOSE and -P options

A brief overview of container networking

Like any computing node, the Docker containers need to be networked, in order to be found and accessible by other containers and clients. In a network, generally, any node is being identified through its IP address. Besides, the IP address is a unique mechanism for any client to reach out to the services offered by any server node. Docker internally uses Linux capabilities to provide network connectivity to containers. In this section, we are going to learn about the container's IP address assignment and the procedure to retrieve the container's IP address.

The Docker engine seamlessly selects and assigns an IP address to a container with no intervention from the user, when it gets launched. Well, you might be puzzled on how Docker selects an IP address for a container, and this puzzle is answered in two parts, which is as follows:

1. During the installation, Docker creates a virtual interface with the name docker0 on the Docker host. It also selects a private IP address range, and assigns an address from the selected range to the docker0 virtual interface. This selected IP address is always outside the range of the Docker host IP address in order to avoid an IP address conflict.

2. Later, when we spin up a container, the Docker engine selects an unused IP address from the IP address range selected for the docker0 virtual interface. Then, the engine assigns this IP address to the freshly spun container.

Docker, by default, selects the IP address 172.17.42.1/16, or one of the IP addresses that is within the range 172.17.0.0 to 172.17.255.255. Docker will select a different private IP address range if there is a direct conflict with the 172.17.x.x addresses. Perhaps, the good old ifconfig (the command to display the details of the network interfaces) comes in handy here to find out the IP address assigned to the virtual interface. Let's just run ifconfig with docker0 as an argument, as follows:

```
$ ifconfig docker0
```

The second line of the output will show the assigned IP address and its netmask:

```
inet addr:172.17.42.1  Bcast:0.0.0.0  Mask:255.255.0.0
```

Apparently, from the preceding text, 172.17.42.1 is the IP address assigned to the docker0 virtual interface. The IP address 172.17.42.1 is one of the addresses in the private IP address range from 172.17.0.0 to 172.17.255.255.

It's now imperative that we learn how to find the IP address assigned to a container. The container should be launched in an interactive mode using the -i option. Of course, we can easily find the IP by running the ifconfig command within the container, as shown here:

```
$ sudo docker run -i -t ubuntu:14.04 /bin/bash

root@4b0b567b6019:/# ifconfig
```

The ifconfig command will display the details of all the interfaces in the Docker container, as follows:

```
eth0      Link encap:Ethernet  HWaddr e6:38:dd:23:aa:3f
          inet addr:172.17.0.12  Bcast:0.0.0.0  Mask:255.255.0.0
          inet6 addr: fe80::e438:ddff:fe23:aa3f/64 Scope:Link
          UP BROADCAST RUNNING  MTU:1500  Metric:1
          RX packets:6 errors:0 dropped:2 overruns:0 frame:0
          TX packets:7 errors:0 dropped:0 overruns:0 carrier:0
          collisions:0 txqueuelen:1000
          RX bytes:488 (488.0 B)  TX bytes:578 (578.0 B)


lo        Link encap:Local Loopback
          inet addr:127.0.0.1  Mask:255.0.0.0
          inet6 addr: ::1/128 Scope:Host
          UP LOOPBACK RUNNING  MTU:65536  Metric:1
          RX packets:0 errors:0 dropped:0 overruns:0 frame:0
          TX packets:0 errors:0 dropped:0 overruns:0 carrier:0
          collisions:0 txqueuelen:0
          RX bytes:0 (0.0 B)  TX bytes:0 (0.0 B)
```

Evidently, the preceding output of the ifconfig command shows that the Docker engine has virtualized two network interfaces for the container, which are as follows:

- The first one is an eth0 (Ethernet) interface for which the Docker engine assigned the IP address 172.17.0.12. Obviously, this address also falls within the same IP address range of the docker0 virtual interface. Besides, the address assigned to the eth0 interface is used for intra-container communication and host-to-container communication.

- The second interface is the lo (Loopback) interface for which the Docker engine assigned the loopback address 127.0.0.1. The loopback interface is used for local communication within a container.

Easy, isn't it? However, the retrieval of an IP address gets complicated when the container is launched in the detached mode, using the -d option in the docker run subcommand. The primary reason for this complication in the detached mode is that there is no shell prompt to run the ifconfig command. Fortunately, Docker provides a docker inspect subcommand, which is as handy as a Swiss army knife, and allow us to dive deep into the low-level details of the Docker container or image. The docker inspect subcommand generates the requested details in the JSON array format.

Here is a sample run of the docker inspect subcommand on the interactive container that we previously launched. The 4b0b567b6019 container ID is taken from the prompt of the container:

```
$ sudo docker inspect 4b0b567b6019
```

This command generates quite a lot of information about the container. Here, we show some excerpts of the container's network configuration from the output of the docker inspect subcommand:

```
"NetworkSettings": {
        "Bridge": "docker0",
        "Gateway": "172.17.42.1",
        "IPAddress": "172.17.0.12",
        "IPPrefixLen": 16,
        "PortMapping": null,
        "Ports": {}
    },
```

Here, the network configuration lists out the following details:

- **Bridge**: This is the bridge interface to which the container is bound
- **Gateway**: This is the gateway address of the container, which is the address of the bridge interface as well
- **IPAddress**: This is the IP address assigned to the container
- **IPPrefixLen**: This is the IP prefix length, another way of representing the subnet mask
- **PortMapping**: This is the port mapping field, which is now being deprecated, and its value is always null
- **Ports**: This is the ports field that will enumerate all the port binds, which is introduced later in this chapter

There is no doubt that the `docker inspect` subcommand is quite convenient for finding the minute details of a container or an image. However, it's a tiresome job to go through the intimidating details and to find the right information that we are keenly looking for. Perhaps, you can narrow it down to the right information, using the `grep` command. Or even better, the `docker inspect` subcommand, which helps you pick the right field from the JSON array using the `--format` option of the `docker inspect` subcommand.

Notably, in the following example, we use the `--format` option of the `docker inspect` subcommand to retrieve just the IP address of the container. The IP address is accessible through the `.NetworkSettings.IPAddress` field of the JSON array:

```
$ sudo docker inspect \
  --format='{{.NetworkSettings.IPAddress}}' 4b0b567b6019
172.17.0.12
```

Envisaging the Container as a Service

We laid a good foundation of the fundamentals of the Docker technology. In this section, we are going to focus on crafting an image with the HTTP service, launch the HTTP service inside the container using the crafted image, and then, demonstrate the connectivity to the HTTP service running inside the container.

Building an HTTP server image

In this section, we are going to craft a Docker image in order to install `Apache2` on top of the `Ubuntu 14.04` base image, and configure a `Apache HTTP Server` to run as an executable, using the `ENTRYPOINT` instruction.

In *Chapter 3, Building Images*, we illustrated the concept of the Dockerfile to craft an `Apache2` image on top of the `Ubuntu 14.04` base image. Here, in this example, we are going to extend this Dockerfile by setting the `Apache` log path and setting `Apache2` as the default execution application, using the `ENTRYPOINT` instruction. The following is a detailed explanation of the content of `Dockerfile`.

We are going to build an image using `ubuntu:14.04` as the base image, using the `FROM` instruction, as shown in the `Dockerfile` snippet:

```
##########################################
# Dockerfile to build an apache2 image
##########################################
```

```
# Base image is Ubuntu
FROM ubuntu:14.04
```

Set authors' detail using MAINTAINER Instruction

```
# Author: Dr. Peter
MAINTAINER Dr. Peter <peterindia@gmail.com>
```

Using one RUN instruction, we will synchronize the apt repository source list, install the apache2 package, and then clean the retrieved files:

```
# Install apache2 package
RUN apt-get update && \
    apt-get install -y apache2 && \
    apt-get clean
```

Set the Apache log directory path using the ENV instruction:

```
# Set the log directory PATH
ENV APACHE_LOG_DIR /var/log/apache2
```

Now, the final instruction is to launch the apache2 server using the ENTRYPOINT instruction:

```
# Launch apache2 server in the foreground
ENTRYPOINT ["/usr/sbin/apache2ctl", "-D", "FOREGROUND"]
```

In the preceding line, you might be surprised to see the FOREGROUND argument. This is one of the key differences between the traditional and the container paradigm. In the traditional paradigm, the server applications are usually launched in the background either as a service or a daemon because the host system is a general-purpose system. However, in the container paradigm, it is imperative to launch an application in the foreground because the images are crafted for a sole purpose.

Having prescribed the image building instruction in the Dockerfile, now let's move to the next logical step of building the image using the docker build subcommand by naming the image as apache2, as shown here:

```
$ sudo docker build -t apache2 .
```

Let's now do a quick verification of the images using the docker images subcommand:

```
$ sudo docker images
```

As we have seen in the previous chapters, the `docker images` command displays the details of all the images in the Docker host. However, in order to illustrate precisely the images created using the `docker build` subcommand, we highlight the details of `apache2:latest` (the target image) and `ubuntu:14.04` (the base image) from the complete image list, as shown in the following output snippet:

```
apache2            latest           d5526cd1a645        About a
minute ago    232.6 MB

ubuntu             14.04            5506de2b643b        5 days
ago           197.8 MB
```

Having built the HTTP server image, now let's move on to the next session to learn how to run the HTTP service.

Running the HTTP server Image as a Service

In this section, we are going to launch a container using the Apache HTTP server image, we crafted in the previous section. Here, we launch the container in the detached mode (similar to a UNIX daemon process) using the `-d` option of the `docker run` subcommand:

```
$ sudo docker run -d apache2

9d4d3566e55c0b8829086e9be2040751017989a47b5411c9c4f170ab865afcef
```

Having launched the container, let's run the `docker logs` subcommand to see whether our Docker container generates any output on its STDIN (standard input) or STDERR (standard error):

```
$ sudo docker logs \
9d4d3566e55c0b8829086e9be2040751017989a47b5411c9c4f170ab865afcef
```

As we have not fully configured the Apache HTTP server; you will find the following warning, as the output of the `docker logs` subcommand:

```
AH00558: apache2: Could not reliably determine the server's fully
qualified domain name, using 172.17.0.13. Set the 'ServerName'
directive globally to suppress this message
```

From the preceding warning message, it is quite evident that the IP address assigned to this container is `172.17.0.13`.

Connecting to the HTTP service

In the preceding section, from the warning message, we found out that the IP address of the container is 172.17.0.13. On a fully configured HTTP server container, no such warning is available, so let's still run the docker inspect subcommand to retrieve the IP address using the container ID:

```
$ sudo docker inspect \
--format='{{.NetworkSettings.IPAddress}}' \
9d4d3566e55c0b8829086e9be2040751017989a47b5411c9c4f170ab865afcef
172.17.0.13
```

Having found the IP address of the container as 172.17.0.13, let's quickly run a web request on this IP address from the shell prompt of the Docker host, using the wget command. Here, we choose to run the wget command with -qO- in order to run in the quiet mode and also display the retrieved HTML file on the screen:

```
$ wget -qO - 172.17.0.13
```

Here, we are showcasing just the first five lines of the retrieved HTML file:

```
<!DOCTYPE html PUBLIC "-//W3C//DTD XHTML 1.0 Transitional//EN"
"http://www.w3.org/TR/xhtml1/DTD/xhtml1-transitional.dtd">
<html xmlns="http://www.w3.org/1999/xhtml">
  <!--
    Modified from the Debian original for Ubuntu
    Last updated: 2014-03-19
```

Awesome, isn't it? We got our first service running in a container, and we are able to reach out to our service from our Docker host.

Furthermore, on a plain vanilla Docker installation, the service offered by one container is accessible by any other container within the Docker host. You can go ahead, launch a new Ubuntu container in the interactive mode, install the wget package using apt-get, and run the same wget -qO - 172.17.0.13 command, as we did in the Docker host. Of course, you will see the same output.

Exposing container services

So far, we have successfully launched an HTTP service and accessed the service from the Docker host as well as another container within the same Docker host. Furthermore, as demonstrated in the *Build images from containers* section of *Chapter 2, Handling Docker Containers*, the container is able to successfully install the wget package by making a connection to the publicly available apt repository over the Internet. Nonetheless, the outside world cannot access the service offered by a container by default. At the outset, this might seem like a limitation in the Docker technology. However, the fact of the matter is, the containers are isolated from the outside world by design.

Docker achieves network isolation for the containers by the IP address assignment criteria, as enumerated:

1. Assign a private IP address to the container, which is not reachable from an external network.
2. Assign an IP address to the container outside the host's IP network.

Consequently, the Docker container is not reachable, even from the systems that are connected to the same IP network as the Docker host. This assignment scheme also provides protection from an IP address conflict that might otherwise arise.

Now, you might wonder how to make the services run inside a container that is accessible to the outside world, in other words, exposing container services. Well, Docker bridges this connectivity gap in a classy manner by leveraging the Linux iptables functionality under the hood.

At the frontend, Docker provides two different building blocks to bridge this connectivity gap for its users. One of the building blocks is to bind the container port using the -p (publish a container's port to the host interface) option of the docker run subcommand. Another alternative is to use the combination of the EXPOSE Dockerfile instruction and the -P (publish all exposed ports to the host interfaces) option of the docker run subcommand.

Publishing container ports – the -p option

Docker enables you to publish a service offered inside a container by binding the container's port to the host interface. The -p option of the docker run subcommand enables you to bind a container port to a user-specified or auto-generated port of the Docker host. Thus, any communication destined for the IP address and the port of the Docker host would be forwarded to the port of the container. The -p option, actually, supports the following four formats of arguments:

- <hostPort>:<containerPort>
- <containerPort>
- <ip>:<hostPort>:<containerPort>
- <ip>::<containerPort>

Here, <ip> is the IP address of the Docker host, <hostPort> is the Docker host port number, and <containerPort> is the port number of the container. Here, in this section, we present you with the -p <hostPort>:<containerPort> format and introduce other formats in the succeeding sections.

In order to understand the port binding process better, let's reuse the apache2 HTTP server image that we crafted previously, and spin up a container using a -p option of the docker run subcommand. The port 80 is the published port of the HTTP service, and as the default behavior, our apache2 HTTP server is also available on port 80. Here, in order to demonstrate this capability, we are going to bind port 80 of the container to port 80 of the Docker host, using the -p <hostPort>:<containerPort> option of the docker run subcommand, as shown in the following command:

```
$ sudo docker run -d -p 80:80 apache2
baddba8afa98725ec85ad953557cd0614b4d0254f45436f9cb440f3f9eeae134
```

Now that we have successfully launched the container, we can connect to our HTTP server using any web browser from any external system (provided it has network connectivity) to reach our Docker host. So far, we have not added any web pages to our apache2 HTTP server image.

Hence, when we connect from a web browser, we will get the following screen, which is nothing but the default page that comes along with the `Ubuntu Apache2` package:

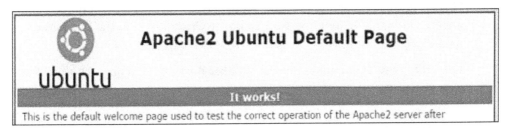

Network Address Translation for containers

In the previous section, we saw how a `-p 80:80` option did the magic, didn't it? Well, in reality, under the hood, the Docker engine achieves this seamless connectivity by automatically configuring the **Network Address Translation (NAT)** rule in the Linux `iptables` configuration files.

To illustrate the automatic configuration of the NAT rule in Linux `iptables`, let's query the Docker hosts `iptables` for its NAT entries, as follows:

```
$ sudo iptables -t nat -L -n
```

The ensuing text is an excerpt from the `iptables` NAT entry, which is automatically added by the Docker engine:

```
Chain DOCKER (2 references)
target      prot opt source              destination
DNAT        tcp  --  0.0.0.0/0           0.0.0.0/0           tcp
dpt:80 to:172.17.0.14:80
```

From the preceding excerpt, it is quite evident that the Docker engine has effectively added a DNAT rule. The following are the details of the DNAT rule:

- The `tcp` keyword signifies that this DNAT rule applies only to the TCP transport protocol.
- The first `0.0.0.0/0` address is a meta IP address of the source address. This address indicates that the connection can originate from any IP address.

- The second `0.0.0.0/0` address is a meta IP address of the destination address on the Docker host. This address indicates that the connection could be made to any valid IP address in the Docker host.

- Finally, `dpt:80 to:172.17.0.14:80` is the forwarding instruction used to forward any TCP activity on port `80` of the Docker host to the IP address `172.17.0.17`, the IP address of our container and port `80`.

  Therefore, any TCP packet that the Docker host receives on port `80` will be forwarded to port `80` of the container.

Retrieving the container port

The Docker engine provides at least three different options to retrieve the containers port binding details. Here, let's first explore the options, and then, move on to dissect the retrieved information. The options are as follows:

- The `docker ps` subcommand always displays the port binding details of a container, as shown here:

```
$ sudo docker ps

CONTAINER ID          IMAGE                 COMMAND
CREATED               STATUS                PORTS
NAMES

baddba8afa98          apache2:latest        "/usr/sbin/apache2ct
26 seconds ago        Up 25 seconds         0.0.0.0:80->80/tcp
furious_carson
```

- The `docker inspect` subcommand is another alternative; however, you have to skim through quite a lot of details. Run the following command:

```
$ sudo docker inspect baddba8afa98
```

The `docker inspect` subcommand displays the port binding related information in three JSON objects, as shown here:

  - The `ExposedPorts` object enumerates all ports that are exposed through the `EXPOSE` instruction in `Dockerfile`, as well as the container ports that are mapped using the `-p` option in the `docker run` subcommand. Since we didn't add the `EXPOSE` instruction in our `Dockerfile`, what we have is just the container port that was mapped using `-p80:80` as an argument to the `docker run` subcommand:

```
"ExposedPorts": {
        "80/tcp": {}
},
```

○ The `PortBindings` object is part of the `HostConfig` object, and this
   object lists out all the port binding done through the -p option in
   the `docker run` subcommand. This object will never list the ports
   exposed through the `EXPOSE` instruction in the `Dockerfile`:

```
"PortBindings": {
            "80/tcp": [
                {
                    "HostIp": "",
                    "HostPort": "80"
                }
            ]
        },
```

○ The `Ports` object of the `NetworkSettings` object has the same level
   of detail, as the preceding `PortBindings` object. However, this
   object encompasses all ports that are exposed through the `EXPOSE`
   instruction in `Dockerfile`, as well as the container ports that are
   mapped using the -p option in the `docker run` subcommand:

```
"NetworkSettings": {
        "Bridge": "docker0",
        "Gateway": "172.17.42.1",
        "IPAddress": "172.17.0.14",
        "IPPrefixLen": 16,
        "PortMapping": null,
        "Ports": {
            "80/tcp": [
                {
                    "HostIp": "0.0.0.0",
                    "HostPort": "80"
                }
            ]
        }
    },
```

Of course, the specific port field can be filtered using the --format option of
the `docker inspect` subcommand.

- The `docker port` subcommand enables you to retrieve the port binding on the Docker host by specifying the container's port number:

```
$ sudo docker port baddba8afa98 80
0.0.0.0:80
```

Evidently, in all the preceding output excerpts, the information that stands out is the IP address `0.0.0.0` and the port number `80`. The IP address `0.0.0.0` is a meta address, which represents all the IP addresses configured on the Docker host. In effect, the containers port `80` is bound to all the valid IP addresses on the Docker host. Therefore, the HTTP service is accessible through any of the valid IP addresses configured on the Docker host.

Binding a container to a specific IP address

Until now, with the method that we have learnt, the containers always get bound to all the IP addresses configured in the Docker host. However, you may want to offer different services on different IP addresses. In other words, a specific IP address and port would be configured to offer a particular service. We can achieve this in Docker using the `-p <ip>:<hostPort>:<containerPort>` option of the `docker run` subcommand, as shown in the following example:

```
$ sudo docker run -d -p 198.51.100.73:80:80 apache2
92f107537bebd48e8917ea4f4788bf3f57064c8c996fc23ea0fd8ea49b4f3335
```

Here, the IP address must be a valid IP address on the Docker host. If the specified IP address is not a valid IP address on the Docker host, the container launch will fail with an error message, as follows:

```
2014/11/09 10:22:10 Error response from daemon: Cannot start
container
99db8d30b284c0a0826d68044c42c370875d2c3cad0b87001b858ba78e9de53b:
Error starting userland proxy: listen tcp 198.51.100.73:80: bind:
cannot assign requested address
```

Now, let's quickly review the port mapping as well as the NAT entry for the preceding example.

The following text is an excerpt from the output of the `docker ps` subcommand that shows the details of this container:

```
92f107537beb         apache2:latest         "/usr/sbin/apache2ct    About
a minute ago    Up About a minute    198.51.100.73:80->80/tcp
boring_ptolemy
```

The following text is an excerpt from the output of the iptables -n nat -L -n command that shows the DNAT entry created for this container:

```
DNAT     tcp -- 0.0.0.0/0        198.51.100.73     tcp dpt:80
to:172.17.0.15:80
```

After reviewing both the output of the docker run subcommand and the DNAT entry of iptables, you will realize how elegantly the Docker engine has configured the service offered by the container on the IP address 198.51.100.73 and port 80 of the Docker host.

Auto-generating the Docker host port

The Docker containers are innately lightweight and due to their lightweight nature, you can run multiple containers with the same, or different services on a single Docker host. Particularly, auto scaling of the same service across several containers based on demand, is the need of IT infrastructure today. Here, in this section, you will be informed about the challenge in spinning up multiple containers with the same service, and also Docker's way of addressing this challenge.

Earlier in this chapter, we launched a container using apache2 http server by binding it to port 80 of the Docker host. Now, if we attempt to launch one more container with the same port 80 binding, the container would fail to start with an error message, as you can see in the following example:

```
$ sudo docker run -d -p 80:80 apache2

6f01f485ab3ce81d45dc6369316659aed17eb341e9ad0229f66060a8ba4a2d0e

2014/11/03 23:28:07 Error response from daemon: Cannot start
container
6f01f485ab3ce81d45dc6369316659aed17eb341e9ad0229f66060a8ba4a2d0e:
Bind for 0.0.0.0:80 failed: port is already allocated
```

Obviously, in the preceding example, the container failed to start because the previous container is already mapped to 0.0.0.0 (all the IP addresses of the Docker host) and port 80. In the TCP/IP communication model, the combination of the IP address, port, and the Transport Protocols (TCP, UDP, and so on) has to be unique.

We could have overcome this issue by manually choosing the Docker host port number (for instance, -p 81:80 or -p 8081:80). Though this is an excellent solution, it does not perform well to auto-scaling scenarios. Instead, if we give the control to Docker, it would auto-generate the port number on the Docker host. This port number generation is achieved by underspecifying the Docker host port number, using the -p <containerPort> option of the docker run subcommand, as shown in the following example:

```
$ sudo docker run -d -p 80 apache2
ea3e0d1b18cff40ffcddd2bf077647dc94bceffad967b86c1a343bd33187d7a8
```

Having successfully started the new container with the auto-generated port, let's review the port mapping as well as the NAT entry for the preceding example:

- The following text is an excerpt from the output of the docker ps subcommand that shows the details of this container:

```
ea3e0d1b18cf        apache2:latest        "/usr/sbin/apache2ct
5 minutes ago       Up 5 minutes          0.0.0.0:49158->80/tcp
nostalgic_morse
```

- The following text is an excerpt from the output of the iptables -n nat -L -n command that shows the DNAT entry created for this container:

```
DNAT    tcp -- 0.0.0.0/0        0.0.0.0/0        tcp dpt:49158
to:172.17.0.18:80
```

After reviewing both the output of the docker run subcommand and the DNAT entry of iptables, what stands out is the port number 49158. The port number 49158 is niftily auto-generated by the Docker engine on the Docker host, with the help of the underlying operating system. Besides, the meta IP address 0.0.0.0 implies that the service offered by the container is accessible from outside, through any of the valid IP addresses configured on the Docker host.

You may have a use case where you want to auto-generate the port number. However, if you still want to restrict the service to a particular IP address of the Docker host, you can use the -p <IP>::<containerPort> option of the docker run subcommand, as shown in the following example:

```
$ sudo docker run -d -p 198.51.100.73::80 apache2
6b5de258b3b82da0290f29946436d7ae307c8b72f22239956e453356532ec2a7
```

In the preceding two scenarios, the Docker engine auto-generated the port number on the Docker host and exposed it to the outside world. The general norm for network communication is to expose any service through a predefined port number so that anybody can know the IP address, and the port number can easily access the offered service. Whereas, here, the port numbers are auto-generated and as a result, the outside world cannot directly reach the offered service. So, the primary purpose of this method of container creation is to achieve auto-scaling, and the container created in this fashion would be interfaced with a proxy or load balance service on a predefined port.

Port binding using EXPOSE and the -P option

So far, we have discussed the four distinct methods to publish a service running inside a container to the outside world. In all these four methods, the port binding decision is taken during the container launch time, and the image has no information about the ports on which the service is being offered. It has worked well so far because the image is being built by us, and we are pretty much aware of the port in which the service is being offered. However, in the case of third-party images, the port usage inside a container has to be published unambiguously. Besides, if we build images for third-party consumption or even for our own use, it is a good practice to explicitly state the ports in which the container offers its service. Perhaps, the image builders could ship a readme document along with the image. However, it is even better to embed the port details in the image itself so that you can easily find the port details from the image both manually as well as through automated scripts.

The Docker technology allows us to embed the port information using the EXPOSE instruction in the Dockerfile, which we introduced in *Chapter 3, Building Images*. Here, let's edit the Dockerfile we used to build the apache2 HTTP server image earlier in this chapter, and add an EXPOSE instruction, as shown in the following code. The default port for the HTTP service is port 80, hence port 80 is exposed:

```
##########################################
# Dockerfile to build an apache2 image
##########################################
# Base image is Ubuntu
FROM ubuntu:14.04
# Author: Dr. Peter
MAINTAINER Dr. Peter <peterindia@gmail.com>
# Install apache2 package
RUN apt-get update && \
```

```
        apt-get install -y apache2 && \
        apt-get clean
# Set the log directory PATH
ENV APACHE_LOG_DIR /var/log/apache2
# Expose port 80
EXPOSE 80
# Launch apache2 server in the foreground
ENTRYPOINT ["/usr/sbin/apache2ctl", "-D", "FOREGROUND"]
```

Now that we have added the EXPOSE instruction to our Dockerfile, let's move to the next step of building the image using the docker build command. Here, let's reuse the image name apache2, as shown here:

```
$ sudo docker build -t apache2 .
```

Having successfully built the image, let's inspect the image to verify the effects of the EXPOSE instruction to the image. As we learnt earlier, we can resort to the docker inspect subcommand, as shown here:

```
$ sudo docker inspect apache2
```

On close review of the output generated by the preceding command, you will realize that Docker stores the exposed port information in the ExposedPorts field of the Config object. The following is an excerpt to show how the exposed port information is being displayed:

```
"ExposedPorts": {
            "80/tcp": {}
        },
```

Alternatively, you can apply the format option to the docker inspect subcommand in order to narrow down the output to very specific information. In this case, the ExposedPorts field of the Config object is shown in the following example:

```
$ sudo docker inspect --format='{{.Config.ExposedPorts}}' \
    apache2
map[80/tcp:map[]]
```

To resume our discussion on the EXPOSE instruction, we can now spin up containers using an apache2 image, that we just crafted. Yet, the EXPOSE instruction by itself cannot create port binding on the Docker host. In order to create port binding for the port declared using the EXPOSE instruction, the Docker engine provides a -P option in the docker run subcommand.

In the following example, a container is launched from the apache2 image, which was rebuilt earlier. Here, the -d option is used to launch the container in the detached mode, and the -P option is used to create the port binding in the Docker host for all the ports declared, using the EXPOSE instruction in the Dockerfile:

```
$ sudo docker run -d -P apache2
fdb1c8d68226c384ab4f84882714fec206a73fd8c12ab57981fbd874e3fa9074
```

Now that we have started the new container with the image that was created using the EXPOSE instruction, like the previous containers, let's review the port mapping as well as the NAT entry for the preceding example:

- The following text is an excerpt from the output of the docker ps subcommand that shows the details of this container:

```
ea3e0d1b18cf        apache2:latest        "/usr/sbin/apache2ct
5 minutes ago       Up 5 minutes          0.0.0.0:49159->80/tcp
nostalgic_morse
```

- The following text is an excerpt from the output of the iptables -t nat -L -n command that shows the DNAT entry created for this container:

```
DNAT     tcp -- 0.0.0.0/0        0.0.0.0/0        tcp dpt:49159
to:172.17.0.19:80
```

The -P option of the docker run subcommand does not take any additional arguments, such as an IP address or a port number; consequently, fine tuning of the port binding is not possible, such as the -p option of the docker run subcommand. You can always resort to the -p option of the docker run subcommand if fine tuning of the port binding is critical to you.

Summary

Containers do not deliver anything in an isolated or solo way substantially. They need to be systematically built and provided with a network interface along with a port number. This leads to a standardized exposition of containers to the outside world, facilitating other hosts or containers to find, bind, and leverage their unique capabilities on any network. Thus, network-accessibility is paramount for containers to get noticed and utilized in innumerable ways. This chapter is dedicated to showcasing how containers are being designed and deployed as a service, and how the aspect of container networking comes in handy by precisely and profusely empowering the peculiar world of container services as the days unfold. In the forthcoming chapters, we will deal and dwell at length on the various capabilities of Docker containers in software-intensive IT environments.

Sharing Data with Containers

7

Do one thing at a time and do it well, is one of the successful mantras of the information technology (IT) sector for quite a long time now. This widely used tenet fits nicely with the building and exposing of Docker containers too and is being prescribed as one of the best practices to avail the originally envisaged benefits of the Docker-inspired containerization paradigm. That is, inscribe a single application along with its direct dependencies and libraries inside a Docker container in order to ensure the container's independence, self-sufficiency, and maneuverability. Let's see why containers are that important:

- **The temporal nature of containers**: The container typically lives as long as the application lives and vice versa. However, this has some negative implications for the application data. It is natural that applications go through a variety of changes in order to accommodate both businesses, as well as technical changes, even in their production environments. There are other causes, such as application malfunction, version changes, application maintenance, and so on, for applications to be updated and upgraded consistently. In the case of a general-purpose computing model, even when an application dies for any reason, the persistent data associated with this application would be preserved in the filesystem. However, in the case of the container paradigm, the application upgrades are usually performed by crafting a new container with the newer version of the application, by discarding the old one. Similarly, when an application malfunctions, a new container needs to be launched and the old one has to be discarded. To sum it up, containers are temporal in nature.

- **The need for business continuity**: In the container landscape, the complete execution environment, including its data files are usually bundled and encapsulated inside the container. For any reason, when a container gets discarded, the application data files also perish along with the container. However, in order to provide a seamless service, these application data files must be preserved outside the container and passed on to the container that will be continuing with the service. Some application data files, such as the log files, need to be accessed outside the container for various posterior-analyses. The Docker technology addresses this file persistence issue very innovatively through a new building block called data volume.

In this chapter, we will cover the following topics:

- Data volume
- Sharing host data
- Sharing data between containers
- The avoidable common pitfalls

The data volume

The data volume is the fundamental building block of data sharing in the Docker environment. Before getting into the details of data sharing, it is imperative to gain a good understanding of the Data Volume concept. Until now, all the files that we created in an image or a container are part and parcel of the Union filesystem. However, the data volume is part of the Docker host filesystem, and it simply gets mounted inside the container.

A data volume can be inscribed in a Docker image using the VOLUME instruction of the Dockerfile. Also, it can be prescribed during the launch of a container using the -v option of the docker run subcommand. Here, in the following example, the implication of the VOLUME instruction in the Dockerfile is illustrated in detail, in the following steps:

1. Create a very simple Dockerfile with the instruction of the base image (ubuntu:14.04) and the data volume (/MountPointDemo):

   ```
   FROM ubuntu:14.04
   VOLUME /MountPointDemo
   ```

2. Build the image with the name mount-point-demo using the docker build subcommand:

   ```
   $ sudo docker build -t mount-point-demo .
   ```

3. Having built the image, let's quickly inspect the image for our data volume using the `docker inspect` subcommand:

```
$ sudo docker inspect mount-point-demo
[{
    "Architecture": "amd64",
... TRUNCATED OUTPUT ...
        "Volumes": {
            "/MountPointDemo": {}
        },
... TRUNCATED OUTPUT ...
```

Evidently, in the preceding output, the data volume is inscribed in the image itself.

4. Now, let's launch an interactive container using the `docker run` subcommand from the earlier crafted image, as shown in the following command:

```
$ sudo docker run --rm -it mount-point-demo
```

From the container's prompt, let's check the presence of the data volume using the `ls -ld` command:

```
root@8d22f73b5b46:/# ls -ld /MountPointDemo
drwxr-xr-x 2 root root 4096 Nov 18 19:22 /MountPointDemo
```

As mentioned earlier, the data volume is part of the Docker host filesystem and it gets mounted, as shown in the following command:

```
root@8d22f73b5b46:/# mount
... TRUNCATED OUTPUT ...
/dev/disk/by-uuid/721cedbd-57b1-4bbd-9488-ec3930862cf5 on
/MountPointDemo type ext3
(rw,noatime,nobarrier,errors=remount-ro,data=ordered)
... TRUNCATED OUTPUT ...
```

5. In this section, we inspected the image to find out about the data volume declaration in the image. Now that we have launched the container, let's inspect the container's data volume using the `docker inspect` subcommand with the container ID as its argument in a different terminal. We created a few containers previously and for this purpose, let's take the container ID `8d22f73b5b46` directly from the container's prompt:

```
$ sudo docker inspect 8d22f73b5b46
... TRUNCATED OUTPUT ...
```

```
    "Volumes": {

        "/MountPointDemo":
"/var/lib/docker/vfs/dir/737e0355c5d81c96a99d41d1b9f540c2a2120
00661633ceea46f2c298a45f128"

    },

    "VolumesRW": {

        "/MountPointDemo": true

    }

}
```

Apparently, here, the data volume is mapped to a directory in the Docker host, and the directory is mounted in read-write mode. This directory is created by the Docker engine automatically during the container launch time.

So far, we have seen the implication of the VOLUME instruction in the Dockerfile, and how Docker manages the data volume. Like the VOLUME instruction of the Dockerfile, we can use the -v <container mount point path> option of the docker run subcommand, as shown in the following command:

```
$ sudo docker run -v /MountPointDemo -it ubuntu:14.04
```

Having launched the container, we encourage you to try the ls -ld / MountPointDemo and mount commands in the newly launched container, and then also, inspect the container, as shown in the preceding step, step 5.

In both the scenarios described here, the Docker engine automatically creates the directory under /var/lib/docker/vfs/ and mounts it to the container. When a container is removed using the docker rm subcommand, the Docker engine does not remove the directory that was automatically created during the container launch time. This behavior is innately designed to preserve the state of the container's application that was stored in the directory. If you want to remove the directory that was automatically created by the Docker engine, you can do so while removing the container by providing a -v option to the docker rm subcommand, on an already stopped container:

```
$ sudo docker rm -v 8d22f73b5b46
```

If the container is still running, then you can remove the container as well as the auto-generated directory by adding a -f option to the previous command:

```
$ sudo docker rm -fv 8d22f73b5b46
```

We have taken you through the techniques and tips to auto-generate a directory in the Docker host and mount it to the data volume in the container. However, with the -v option of the docker run subcommand, a user-defined directory can be mounted to the data volume. In such cases, the Docker engine would not auto-generate any directory.

 The system-generated directory has a caveat of directory leak. In other words, if you forget to delete the system-generated directories, you may face some unwanted issues. For further information, you can read the *Avoiding common pitfalls* section in this chapter.

Sharing host data

Earlier, we described the steps towards creating a data volume in a Docker image using the VOLUME instruction in the Dockerfile. However, Docker does not provide any mechanism to mount the host directory or file during the build time in order to ensure the Docker images are portable. The only provision Docker provides is to mount the host directory or file to a container's data volume during the container's launch time. Docker exposes the host directory or file mounting facility through the -v option of the docker run subcommand. The –v option has three different formats enumerated as follows:

1. -v <container mount path>
2. -v <host path>/<container mount path>
3. -v <host path>/<container mount path>:<read write mode>

The <host path> is an absolute path in the Docker host, <container mount path> is an absolute path in the container filesystem, and <read write mode> can be either read-only (ro) or read-write (rw) mode. The first -v <container mount path> format has already been explained in the *Data Volume* section in this chapter, as a method to create a mount point during the container launch time. The second and third options enable us to mount a file or directory from the Docker host to the container mount point.

We would like to dig deeper to gain a better understanding of the host's data sharing through a couple of examples. In the first example, we will demonstrate how to share a directory between the Docker host and the container, and in the second example, we will demonstrate file sharing.

Here, in the first example, we mount a directory from the Docker host to a container, perform a few basic file operations on the container, and verify these operations from the Docker host, as detailed in the following steps:

1. First, let's launch an interactive container with the -v option of the docker run subcommand to mount /tmp/hostdir of the Docker host directory to /MountPoint of the container:

   ```
   $ sudo docker run -v /tmp/hostdir:/MountPoint \
                      -it ubuntu:14.04
   ```

    If /tmp/hostdir is not found on the Docker host, the Docker engine will create the directory itself. However, the problem is that the system-generated directory cannot be deleted using the -v option of the docker rm subcommand.

2. Having successfully launched the container, we can check the presence of /MountPoint using the ls command:

   ```
   root@4a018d99c133:/# ls -ld /MountPoint
   drwxr-xr-x 2 root root 4096 Nov 23 18:28 /MountPoint
   ```

3. Now, we can proceed to checking the mount details using the mount command:

   ```
   root@4a018d99c133:/# mount
   ... TRUNCATED OUTPUT ...
   /dev/disk/by-uuid/721cedbd-57b1-4bbd-9488-ec3930862cf5 on
   /MountPoint type ext3 (rw,noatime,nobarrier,errors=remount-
   ro,data=ordered)
   ... TRUNCATED OUTPUT ...
   ```

4. Here, we are going to validate /MountPoint, change to the /MountPoint directory using the cd command, create a few files using the touch command, and list the files using the ls command, as shown in the following script:

   ```
   root@4a018d99c133:/# cd /MountPoint/
   root@4a018d99c133:/MountPoint# touch {a,b,c}
   root@4a018d99c133:/MountPoint# ls -l
   total 0
   -rw-r--r-- 1 root root 0 Nov 23 18:39 a
   -rw-r--r-- 1 root root 0 Nov 23 18:39 b
   -rw-r--r-- 1 root root 0 Nov 23 18:39 c
   ```

5. It might be worth the effort to verify the files in the `/tmp/hostdir` Docker host directory using the `ls` command on a new terminal, as our container is running in an interactive mode on the existing terminal:

```
$ sudo  ls -l /tmp/hostdir/

total 0

-rw-r--r-- 1 root root 0 Nov 23 12:39 a

-rw-r--r-- 1 root root 0 Nov 23 12:39 b

-rw-r--r-- 1 root root 0 Nov 23 12:39 c
```

   Here, we can see the same set of files, as we can see in step 4. However, you might have noticed the difference in the time stamp of the files. This time difference is due to the time-zone difference between the Docker host and the container.

6. Finally, let's run the `docker inspect` subcommand with the container ID `4a018d99c133` as an argument to see whether the directory mapping is set up between the Docker host and the container mount point, as shown in the following command:

```
$ sudo docker inspect \
                --format={{.Volumes}}  4a018d99c133
map[/MountPoint:/tmp/hostdir]
```

   Apparently, in the preceding output of the `docker inspect` subcommand, the `/tmp/hostdir` directory of the Docker host is mounted on the `/MountPoint` mount point of the container.

For the second example, we can mount a file from the Docker host to a container, update the file from the container, and verify these operations from the Docker host, as detailed in the following steps:

1. In order to mount a file from the Docker host to the container, the file must preexist in the Docker host. Otherwise, the Docker engine will create a new directory with the specified name, and mount it as a directory. We can start by creating a file on the Docker host using the `touch` command:

```
$ touch /tmp/hostfile.txt
```

2. Launch an interactive container with the `-v` option of the `docker run` subcommand to mount the `/tmp/hostfile.txt` Docker host file to the container as `/tmp/mntfile.txt`:

```
$ sudo docker run -v /tmp/hostfile.txt:/mountedfile.txt \
                -it ubuntu:14.04
```

3. Having successfully launched the container, now let's check the presence of /mountedfile.txt using the ls command:

```
root@d23a15527eeb:/# ls -l /mountedfile.txt
-rw-rw-r-- 1 1000 1000 0 Nov 23 19:33 /mountedfile.txt
```

4. Then, proceed to check the mount details using the mount command:

```
root@d23a15527eeb:/# mount
... TRUNCATED OUTPUT ...
/dev/disk/by-uuid/721cedbd-57b1-4bbd-9488-ec3930862cf5 on
/mountedfile.txt type ext3
(rw,noatime,nobarrier,errors=remount-ro,data=ordered)
... TRUNCATED OUTPUT ...
```

5. Then, update some text to /mountedfile.txt using the echo command:

```
root@d23a15527eeb:/# echo "Writing from Container" \
         > mountedfile.txt
```

6. Meanwhile, switch to a different terminal in the Docker host, and print the /tmp/hostfile.txt Docker host file using the cat command:

```
$ cat /tmp/hostfile.txt
Writing from Container
```

7. Finally, run the docker inspect subcommand with the container ID d23a15527eeb as it's argument to see the file mapping between the Docker host and the container mount point:

```
$ sudo docker inspect \
                --format={{.Volumes}} d23a15527eeb
map[/mountedfile.txt:/tmp/hostfile.txt]
```

From the preceding output, it is evident that the /tmp/hostfile.txt file from the Docker host is mounted as /mountedfile.txt inside the container.

 In the case of file sharing between the Docker host and container, the file must exist before launching the container. However, in the case of directory sharing, if the directory does not exist in the Docker host, then the Docker engine would create a new directory in the Docker host, as explained earlier.

The practicality of host data sharing

In the previous chapter, we launched an HTTP service in a Docker container. However, if you remember correctly, the log file for the HTTP service is still inside the container, and it cannot be accessed directly from the Docker host. Here, in this section, we elucidate the procedure of accessing the log files from the Docker host in a step-by-step manner:

1. Let's begin with launching an Apache2 HTTP service container by mounting the /var/log/myhttpd directory of the Docker host to the /var/log/apache2 directory of the container, using the –v option of the docker run subcommand. In this example, we are leveraging the apache2 image, which we had built in the previous chapter, by invoking the following command:

   ```
   $ sudo docker run -d -p 80:80 \
           -v /var/log/myhttpd:/var/log/apache2 apache2
   9c2f0c0b126f21887efaa35a1432ba7092b69e0c6d
   523ffd50684e27eeab37ac
   ```

   If you recall the Dockerfile in *Chapter 6, Running Services in a Container*, the APACHE_LOG_DIR environment variable is set to the /var/log/apache2 directory, using the ENV instruction. This would make the Apache2 HTTP service route all log messages to the /var/log/apache2 data volume.

2. Once the container is launched, we can change the directory to /var/log/ myhttpd on the Docker host:

   ```
   $ cd /var/log/myhttpd
   ```

3. Perhaps, a quick check of the files present in the /var/log/myhttpd directory is appropriate here:

   ```
   $ ls -1
   access.log
   error.log
   other_vhosts_access.log
   ```

   Here, the access.log contains all the access requests handled by the Apache2 HTTP server. The error.log is a very important log file, where our HTTP server records the errors it encounters while processing any HTTP requests. The other_vhosts_access.log file is the virtual host log, which will always be empty in our case.

4. We can display the content of all the log files in the /var/log/myhttpd directory using the tail command with the -f option:

```
$ tail -f *.log
==> access.log <==


==> error.log <==

AH00558: apache2: Could not reliably determine the server's
fully qualified domain name, using 172.17.0.17. Set the
'ServerName' directive globally to suppress this message
[Thu Nov 20 17:45:35.619648 2014] [mpm_event:notice] [pid
16:tid 140572055459712] AH00489: Apache/2.4.7 (Ubuntu)
configured -- resuming normal operations
[Thu Nov 20 17:45:35.619877 2014] [core:notice] [pid 16:tid
140572055459712] AH00094: Command line: '/usr/sbin/apache2 -D
FOREGROUND'
==> other_vhosts_access.log <==
```

The tail -f command will run continuously and display the content of the files, as soon as they get updated. Here, both access.log and other_vhosts_access.log are empty, and there are a few error messages on the error.log file. Apparently, these error logs are generated by the HTTP service running inside the container. The logs are then stocked in the Docker host directory, which is mounted during the launch time of the container.

5. As we continue to run tail -f *, let's connect to the HTTP service from a web browser running inside the container, and observe the log files:

```
==> access.log <==
111.111.172.18 - - [20/Nov/2014:17:53:38 +0000] "GET /
HTTP/1.1" 200 3594 "-" "Mozilla/5.0 (Windows NT 6.1; WOW64)
AppleWebKit/537.36 (KHTML, like Gecko) Chrome/39.0.2171.65
Safari/537.36"

111.111.172.18 - - [20/Nov/2014:17:53:39 +0000] "GET
/icons/ubuntu-logo.png HTTP/1.1" 200 3688
"http://111.71.123.110/" "Mozilla/5.0 (Windows NT 6.1; WOW64)
AppleWebKit/537.36 (KHTML, like Gecko) Chrome/39.0.2171.65
Safari/537.36"

111.111.172.18 - - [20/Nov/2014:17:54:21 +0000] "GET
/favicon.ico HTTP/1.1" 404 504 "-" "Mozilla/5.0 (Windows NT
6.1; WOW64) AppleWebKit/537.36 (KHTML, like Gecko)
Chrome/39.0.2171.65 Safari/537.36"
```

The HTTP service updates the access.log file, which we can manipulate from the host directory mounted through the -v option of the docker run subcommand.

Sharing data between containers

In the previous section, we learnt how seamlessly the Docker engine enables data sharing between the Docker host and the container. Even though it is a very effective solution, it tightly couples the container to the host filesystem. These directories might leave a nasty footprint because the user has to manually remove them once their purpose is met. So, the Docker's prescription to solve this issue is to create data-only containers as a base container, and then mount the Data Volume of that container to other containers using the `--volume-from` option of the `docker run` subcommand.

Data-only containers

The prime responsibility of a data-only container is to preserve the data. Creating a data-only container is very similar to the method illustrated in the data volume section. In addition, the containers are named explicitly for other containers to mount the data volume using the container's name. The container's data volumes are accessible from other containers even when the data-only containers are in the stopped state. The data-only containers can be created in two ways, as follows:

- During the container's launch time by configuring the data volume and container's name.

- The data volume can also be inscribed with `Dockerfile` during the image-building time, and later the container can be named during the container's launch time.

In the following example, we are launching a data-only container by configuring the container launch with the `-v` and `--name` options of the `docker run` subcommand, as shown here:

```
$ sudo docker run --name datavol \
                -v /DataMount \
                busybox:latest /bin/true
```

Here, the container is launched from the `busybox` image, which is widely used for its smaller footprint. Here, we choose to execute the `/bin/true` command because we don't intend to do any operations on the container. Therefore, we named the container `datavol` using the `--name` option and created a new `/DataMount` data volume using the `-v` option of the `docker run` subcommand. The `/bin/true` command exits immediately with the exit status `0`, which in turn will stop the container and continue to be in the stopped state.

Mounting data volume from other containers

The Docker engine provides a nifty interface to mount (share) the data volume from one container to another. Docker makes this interface available through the `--volumes-from` option of the `docker run` subcommand. The `--volumes-from` option takes a container name or container ID as its input and automatically mounts all the data volumes available on the specified container. Docker allows you to mount multiple containers with the data volume using the `--volumes-from` option multiple times.

Here is a practical example that demonstrates how to mount the data volume from another container and showcases the data volume mount process, step by step.

1. We begin with launching an interactive Ubuntu container by mounting the data volume from the data-only container (`datavol`), which we launched in the previous section, as explained here:

   ```
   $ sudo docker run -it \
                   --volumes-from datavol \
                   ubuntu:latest /bin/bash
   ```

2. Now from the container's prompt, let's verify the data volume mounts using the `mount` command:

   ```
   root@e09979cacec8:/# mount
   . . . TRUNCATED OUTPUT . . .
   /dev/disk/by-uuid/32a56fe0-7053-4901-ae7e-24afe5942e91 on
   /DataMount type ext3 (rw,noatime,nobarrier,errors=remount-
   ro,data=ordered)
   . . . TRUNCATED OUTPUT . . .
   ```

   Here, we successfully mounted the data volume from the `datavol` data-only container.

3. Next, we need to inspect the data volume of this container from another terminal using the `docker inspect` subcommand:

   ```
   $ sudo docker inspect   e09979cacec8
   . . . TRUNCATED OUTPUT . . .
     "Volumes": {
       "/DataMount": "/var/lib/docker/vfs/dir/62f5a3314999e5aaf485fc6
   92ae07b3cbfacb
   ca9815d8071f519c1a836c0f01e"
   ```

```
    },
      "VolumesRW": {
        "/DataMount": true
      }
    }
```

Evidently, the data volume from the `datavol` data-only container is mounted as if they were mounted directly on to this container.

We can mount a data volume from another container and also showcase the mount points. We can make the mounted data volume work by sharing data between containers using the data volume, as demonstrated here:

1. Let's reuse the container that we launched in the previous example and create a `/DataMount/testfile` file in the data volume `/DataMount` by writing some text to the file, as shown here:

```
root@e09979cacec8:/# echo \
            "Data Sharing between Container" > \
            /DataMount/testfile
```

2. Just spin off a container to display the text that we wrote in the previous step, using the `cat` command:

```
$ sudo docker run --rm \
                --volumes-from datavol \
                busybox:latest cat /DataMount/testfile
```

The following is the typical output of the preceding command:

```
Data Sharing between Container
```

Evidently, the preceding output `Data Sharing between Container` of our newly containerized `cat` command is the text that we have written in `/DataMount/testfile` of the `datavol` container in step 1.

Cool, isn't it? You can share data seamlessly between containers by sharing the data volumes. Here, in this example, we used data-only containers as the base container for data sharing. However, Docker allows us to share any type of data volumes and to mount data volumes one after another, as depicted here:

```
$ sudo docker run --name vol1 --volumes-from datavol \
        busybox:latest /bin/true
$ sudo docker run --name vol2 --volumes-from vol1 \
        busybox:latest /bin/true
```

Here, in the `vol1` container, we can mount the data volume from the `datavol` container. Then, in the `vol2` container, we mounted the data volume from the `vol1` container, which is originally from the `datavol` container.

The practicality of data sharing between containers

Earlier, in this chapter, we learnt the mechanism of accessing the log files of the Apache2 HTTP service from the Docker host. Although it was fairly convenient to share data by mounting the Docker host directory to a container, later we came to realise that data can be shared between containers by just using the data volumes. So here, we are bringing in a twist to the method of the Apache2 HTTP service log handling by sharing data between containers. To share log files between containers, we will spin off the following containers as enlisted in the following steps:

1. First, a data-only container that would expose the data volume to other containers.

2. Then, an Apache2 HTTP service container leveraging the data volume of the data-only container.

3. A container to view the log files generated by our Apache2 HTTP service.

 NOTE: If you are running any HTTP service on the port number 80 of your Docker host machine, pick any other unused port number for the following example. If not, first stop the HTTP service, then proceed with the example in order to avoid any port conflict.

Now, we meticulously walk you through the steps to craft the respective images and launch the containers to view the log files, as illustrated here:

1. Here, we begin with crafting a `Dockerfile` with the `/var/log/apache2` data volume using the `VOLUME` instruction. The `/var/log/apache2` data volume is a direct mapping to `APACHE_LOG_DIR`, the environment variable set in the `Dockerfile` in *Chapter 6, Running Services in a Container*, using the `ENV` instruction:

    ```
    ####################################################
    # Dockerfile to build a LOG Volume for Apache2 Service
    ####################################################
    ```

```
# Base image is BusyBox
FROM busybox:latest
# Author: Dr. Peter
MAINTAINER Dr. Peter <peterindia@gmail.com>
# Create a data volume at /var/log/apache2, which is
# same as the log directory PATH set for the apache image
VOLUME /var/log/apache2
# Execute command true
CMD ["/bin/true"]
```

Since this `Dockerfile` is crafted to launch data-only containers, the default execution command is set to `/bin/true`.

2. We will continue to build a Docker image with the name `apache2log` from the preceding `Dockerfile` using `docker build`, as presented here:

```
$ sudo docker build -t apache2log .

Sending build context to Docker daemon   2.56 kB

Sending build context to Docker daemon

Step 0 : FROM busybox:latest

... TRUNCATED OUTPUT ...
```

3. Launch a data-only container from the `apache2log` image using the `docker run` subcommand and name the resulting container `log_vol`, using the `--name` option:

```
$ sudo docker run --name log_vol apache2log
```

Acting on the preceding command, the container will create a data volume in `/var/log/apache2` and move it to a stop state.

4. Meanwhile, you can run the `docker ps` subcommand with the `-a` option to verify the container's state:

```
$ sudo docker ps -a

CONTAINER ID           IMAGE                COMMAND
CREATED                STATUS                       PORTS
NAMES

40332e5fa0ae           apache2log:latest    "/bin/true"
2 minutes ago          Exited (0) 2 minutes ago
log_vol
```

As per the output, the container exits with the exit value `0`.

5. Launch the Apache2 HTTP service using the docker run subcommand. Here, we are reusing the apache2 image we crafted in *Chapter 6, Running Services in a Container*. In this container, we will mount the /var/log/apache2 data volume from log_vol, the data-only container that we launched in step 3, using the --volumes-from option:

```
$ sudo docker run -d -p 80:80 \
                --volumes-from log_vol \
                apache2
7dfbf87e341c320a12c1baae14bff2840e64afcd082dda3094e7cb0a002
3cf42
```

With the successful launch of the Apache2 HTTP service with the /var/log/apache2 data volume mounted from log_vol, we can access the log files using transient containers.

6. Here, we are listing the files stored by the Apache2 HTTP service using a transient container. This transient container is spun off by mounting the /var/log/apache2 data volume from log_vol, and the files in /var/log/apache2 are listed using the ls command. Further, the --rm option of the docker run subcommand is used to remove the container once it is done executing the ls command:

```
$   sudo docker run --rm \
                --volumes-from log_vol
                busybox:latest ls -l /var/log/apache2
total 4
-rw-r--r--    1 root     root             0 Dec  5 15:27
access.log
-rw-r--r--    1 root     root           461 Dec  5 15:27
error.log
-rw-r--r--    1 root     root             0 Dec  5 15:27
other_vhosts_access.log
```

7. Finally, the error log produced by the Apache2 HTTP service is accessed using the tail command, as highlighted in the following command:

```
$ sudo docker run  --rm  \
                --volumes-from log_vol \
                ubuntu:14.04 \
                tail /var/log/apache2/error.log
```

```
AH00558: apache2: Could not reliably determine the server's
fully qualified domain name, using 172.17.0.24. Set the
'ServerName' directive globally to suppress this message

[Fri Dec 05 17:28:12.358034 2014] [mpm_event:notice] [pid
18:tid 140689145714560] AH00489: Apache/2.4.7 (Ubuntu)
configured -- resuming normal operations

[Fri Dec 05 17:28:12.358306 2014] [core:notice] [pid 18:tid
140689145714560] AH00094: Command line: '/usr/sbin/apache2 -D
FOREGROUND'
```

Avoiding common pitfalls

Till now, we discussed how effectively data volumes can be used to share data between the Docker host and the containers as well as between containers. Data sharing using data volumes is turning out to be a very powerful and essential tool in the Docker paradigm. However, it does carry a few pitfalls that are to be carefully identified and eliminated. In this section, we make an attempt to list out a few common issues associated with data sharing and the ways and means to overcome them.

Directory leaks

Earlier in the data volume section, we learnt that the Docker engine automatically creates directories based on the VOLUME instruction in Dockerfile as well as the -v option of the docker run subcommand. We also understood that the Docker engine does not automatically delete these auto-generated directories in order to preserve the state of the application(s) run inside the container. We can force Docker to remove these directories using the -v option of the docker rm subcommand. This process of manual deletion poses two major challenges enumerated as follows:

1. **Undeleted directories:** There could be scenarios where you may intentionally or unintentionally choose not to remove the generated directory while removing the container.

2. **Third-party images:** Quite often, we leverage third-party Docker images that could have been built with the VOLUME instruction. Likewise, we might also have our own Docker images with VOLUME inscribed in it. When we launch containers using such Docker images, the Docker engine will auto-generate the prescribed directories. Since we are not aware of the data volume creation, we may not call the docker rm subcommand with the -v option to delete the auto-generated directory.

In the previously mentioned scenarios, once the associated container is removed, there is no direct way to identify the directories whose containers were removed. Here are a few recommendations on how to avoid this pitfall:

- Always inspect the Docker images using the `docker inspect` subcommand and check whether any data volume is inscribed in the image or not.

- Always run the `docker rm` subcommand with the `-v` option to remove any data volume (directory) created for the container. Even if the data volume is shared by multiple containers, it is still safe to run the `docker rm` subcommand with the `-v` option because the directory associated with the data volume will be deleted only when the last container sharing that data volume is removed.

- For any reason, if you choose to preserve the auto-generated directory, you must keep a clear record so that you can remove them at a later point of time.

- Implement an audit framework that will audit and find out the directories that do not have any container association.

The undesirable effect of data volume

As mentioned earlier, Docker enables us to etch data volumes in a Docker image using the VOLUME instruction during the build time. Nonetheless, the data volumes should never be used to store any data during the build time, otherwise it will result in an unwanted effect.

In this section, we will demonstrate the undesirable effect of using the data volume during the build time by crafting a Dockerfile, and then showcase the implication by building this Dockerfile:

The following are the details of Dockerfile:

1. Build the image using Ubuntu 14.04 as the base image:

   ```
   # Use Ubuntu as the base image
   FROM ubuntu:14.04
   ```

2. Create a /MountPointDemo data volume using the VOLUME instruction:

   ```
   VOLUME /MountPointDemo
   ```

3. Create a file in the /MountPointDemo data volume using the RUN instruction:

   ```
   RUN date > /MountPointDemo/date.txt
   ```

4. Display the file in the /MountPointDemo data volume using the RUN instruction:

```
RUN cat /MountPointDemo/date.txt
```

Proceed to build an image from this Dockerfile using the docker build subcommand, as shown here:

```
$ sudo docker build -t testvol .
Sending build context to Docker daemon  2.56 kB
Sending build context to Docker daemon
Step 0 : FROM ubuntu:14.04
 ---> 9bd07e480c5b
Step 1 : VOLUME /MountPointDemo
 ---> Using cache
 ---> e8b1799d4969
Step 2 : RUN date > /MountPointDemo/date.txt
 ---> Using cache
 ---> 8267e251a984
Step 3 : RUN cat /MountPointDemo/date.txt
 ---> Running in a3e40444de2e
cat: /MountPointDemo/date.txt: No such file or directory
2014/12/07 11:32:36 The command [/bin/sh -c cat
/MountPointDemo/date.txt] returned a non-zero code: 1
```

In the preceding output of the docker build subcommand, you would have noticed that the build fails at step 3 because it cannot find the file created in step 2. Apparently, the file that was created in step 2 vanishes when it reaches step 3. This undesirable effect is due to the approach Docker uses to build its images. An understanding of the Docker image-building process would unravel the mystery.

In the build process, for every instruction in a Dockerfile, the following steps are followed:

1. Create a new container by translating the Dockerfile instruction to an equivalent docker run subcommand

2. Commit the newly-created container to an image

3. Repeat step 1 and step 2, by treating the newly-created image as the base image for step 1.

When a container is committed, it saves the container's filesystem and, deliberately, does not save the data volume's filesystem. Therefore, any data stored in the data volume will be lost in this process. So never use a data volume as storage during the build process.

Summary

For enterprise-scale distributed applications to be distinct in their operations and outputs, data is the most important instrument and ingredient. With IT containerization, the journey takes off in a brisk and bright fashion. IT as well as business software solutions are intelligently containerized through the smart leverage of the Docker engine. However, the original instigation is the need for a faster and flawless realization of application-aware Docker containers, and hence, the data is tightly coupled with the application within the container. However, this closeness brings in some real risks. If the application collapses, then the data is also gone. Also, multiple applications might depend on the same data and hence, data has to be shared across.

In this chapter, we discussed the capabilities of the Docker engine in facilitating the seamless data sharing between the Docker host and container as well as between containers. The data volume is being prescribed as the foundational building block for enabling data sharing among the constituents of the growing Docker ecosystem. In the next chapter, we will explain the concept behind the container orchestration, and see how this complicated aspect gets simplified through a few automated tools. Orchestration is indispensable for realizing composite containers.

8

Orchestrating Containers

In the earlier chapters, we laid down a strong foundation for the need for container networking, how to run a service inside a Docker container, and how to expose this service to the outside world by opening up network ports and other prerequisites. However, recently, there are advanced mechanisms being made available and a few third-party orchestration platforms hitting the market for sagaciously establishing dynamic and decisive linkages between distributed and differently enabled containers in order to compose powerful containers for comprehensively, yet compactly containing process-centric, multi-tiered, and enterprise-class distributed applications. In this extremely diversified yet connected world, the concept of orchestration cannot be kept away from its deserved prominence for long. This chapter is precisely devoted for explaining the nitty-gritty of container orchestration, and its direct role in picking up discrete containers to systematically compose sophisticated containers that are more directly aligned to the varying business expectations and expediencies.

In this chapter, we will discuss the details associated with the following topics:

- Linking containers
- Orchestrating containers
- Container orchestration using the `docker-compose` tool

As mission-critical applications are overwhelmingly being built through loosely coupled, yet highly cohesive components/services destined to run on geographically distributed IT infrastructures and platforms, the concept of composition is getting a lot of attention and attraction. For sustaining the well-begun containerization journey, the orchestration of containers is being prescribed as one of the most critical and crucial requirements in the ensuing instant-on, adaptive, and smart IT era. There are a few proven and promising methods and standards-compliant tools for enabling the enigmatic orchestration goals.

Linking containers

One of the prominent features of the Docker technology is linking containers. That is, cooperating containers can be linked together to offer complex and business-aware services. The linked containers have a kind of source-recipient relationship, wherein the source container gets linked to the recipient container, and the recipient securely receives a variety of information from the source container. However, the source container would know nothing about the recipients to which it is linked to. Another noteworthy feature of linking containers, in a secured setup, is that the linked containers can communicate using secured tunnels without exposing the ports used for the setup, to the external world.

The Docker engine provides the `--link` option in the `docker run` subcommand to link a source container to a recipient container.

The format of the `--link` option is as follows:

```
--link <container>:<alias>
```

Here, `<container>` is the name of the source container and `<alias>` is the name seen by the recipient container. The name of the container must be unique in a Docker host, whereas alias is very specific and local to the recipient container, and hence, the alias need not be unique to the Docker host. This gives a lot of flexibility towards implementing and incorporating functionalities with a fixed source alias name inside the recipient container.

When two containers are linked together, the Docker engine automatically exports a few environment variables to the recipient container. These environment variables have a well-defined naming convention, where the variables are always prefixed with capitalized form of the alias name. For instance, if `src` is the alias name given to the source container, then the exported environment variables would begin with `SRC_`. Docker exports three categories of environment variables, as enumerated here:

1. `NAME`: This is the first category of environment variables. This variable takes the form of `<ALIAS>_NAME`, and it carries the recipient container's hierarchical name as its value. For instance, if the source container's alias is `src` and the recipient container's name is `rec`, then the environment variable and its value would be `SRC_NAME=/rec/src`.

2. `ENV`: This is the second category of environment variables. These variables export the environment variables configured in the source container by the `-e` option of the `docker run` subcommand or the `ENV` instruction of `Dockerfile`. This type of an environment variable takes the form of `<ALIAS>_ENV_<VAR_NAME>`. For instance, if the source container's alias is `src` and the variable name is `SAMPLE`, then the environment variable would be `SRC_ENV_SAMPLE`.

3. PORT: This is the final and third category of environment variables that is used to export the connectivity details of the source container to the recipient. Docker creates a bunch of variables for each port exposed by the source container through the -p option of the `docker run` subcommand or the `EXPOSE` instruction of the `Dockerfile`.

   These variables take the form:

   `*<ALIAS>_PORT_<port>_<protocol>`

   This form is used to share the source's IP address, port, and protocol as an URL. For example, if the source container's alias is `src`, the exposed port is `8080`, the protocol is `tcp`, and the IP address is `172.17.0.2`, then the environment variable and its value would be `SRC_PORT_8080_TCP=tcp://172.17.0.2:8080`. This URL further splits into the following three environment variables:

   ○ `<ALIAS>_PORT_<port>_<protocol>_ADDR`: This form carries the IP address part of the URL (For example: `SRC_PORT_8080_TCP_ADDR=172.17.0.2`)

   ○ `<ALIAS>_PORT_<port>_<protocol>_PORT`: This form carries the port part of the URL (For example: `SRC_PORT_8080_TCP_PORT=8080`)

   ○ `<ALIAS>_PORT_<port>_<protocol>_PROTO`: This form carries the protocol part of the URL (For example: `SRC_PORT_8080_TCP_PROTO=tcp`)

In addition to the preceding environment variables, the Docker engine exports one more variable in this category, that is, of the form `<ALIAS>_PORT`, and its value would be the URL of the lowest number of all the exposed ports of the source container. For instance, if the source container's alias is `src`, the exposed port numbers are `7070`, `8080`, and `80`, the protocol is `tcp`, and the IP address is `172.17.0.2`, then the environment variable and its value would be `SRC_PORT=tcp://172.17.0.2:80`.

Docker exports these auto-generated environment variables in a well-structured format so that they can be easily discovered programmatically. Thus, it becomes very easy for the recipient container to discover the information about the source container. In addition, Docker automatically updates the source IP address and its alias as an entry in the recipient's `/etc/hosts` file.

In this chapter, we will take you deep into the mentioned features provided by the Docker engine for container linkage through a bevy of pragmatic examples.

To start with, let's choose a simple container linking example. Here, we will show you how to establish a linkage between two containers, and transfer some basic information from the source container to the recipient container, as illustrated in the following steps:

1. We begin by launching an interactive container that can be used as a source container for linking, using the following command:

   ```
   $ sudo docker run --rm --name example -it busybox:latest
   ```

   The container is named `example` using the `--name` option. In addition, the `--rm` option is used to clean up the container as soon as you exit from the container.

2. Display the `/etc/hosts` entry of the source container using the `cat` command:

   ```
   / # cat /etc/hosts
   172.17.0.3        a02895551686
   127.0.0.1         localhost
   ::1     localhost ip6-localhost ip6-loopback
   fe00::0 ip6-localnet
   ff00::0 ip6-mcastprefix
   ff02::1 ip6-allnodes
   ff02::2 ip6-allrouters
   ```

   Here, the first entry in the `/etc/hosts` file is the source container's IP address (`172.17.0.3`) and its hostname (`a02895551686`).

3. We will continue to display the environment variables of the source container using the `env` command:

   ```
   / # env
   HOSTNAME=a02895551686
   SHLVL=1
   HOME=/root
   TERM=xterm
   PATH=/usr/local/sbin:/usr/local/bin:/usr/sbin:/usr/bin:/sbin:/bin
   PWD=/
   ```

4. Having launched the source container, from another terminal of the same Docker host, let's launch an interactive recipient container by linking it to our source container using the `--link` option of the `docker run` subcommand, as shown here:

```
$ sudo docker run --rm --link example:ex -it busybox:latest
```

Here, the source container named `example` is linked to the recipient container with `ex` as its alias.

5. Let's display the content of the `/etc/hosts` file of the recipient container using the `cat` command:

```
/ # cat /etc/hosts
172.17.0.4        a17e5578b98e
127.0.0.1         localhost
::1     localhost ip6-localhost ip6-loopback
fe00::0 ip6-localnet
ff00::0 ip6-mcastprefix
ff02::1 ip6-allnodes
ff02::2 ip6-allrouters
172.17.0.3        ex
```

Of course, as always, the first entry of the `/etc/hosts` file is the container's IP address and its hostname. However, the noteworthy entry in the `/etc/hosts` file is the last entry, where the source container's IP address (`172.17.0.3`) and its alias (ex) are added automatically.

6. We will continue to display the recipient container's environment variable using the `env` command:

```
/ # env
HOSTNAME=a17e5578b98e
SHLVL=1
HOME=/root
EX_NAME=/berserk_mcclintock/ex
TERM=xterm
PATH=/usr/local/sbin:/usr/local/bin:/usr/sbin:/usr/bin:/sbin:/bin
PWD=/
```

Apparently, a new `EX_NAME` environment variable is added automatically to `/berserk_mcclintock/ex`, as its value. Here `EX` is the capitalized form of the alias `ex` and `berserk_mcclintock` is the auto-generated name of the recipient container.

7. As a final step, ping the source container using the widely used `ping` command for two counts, and use the alias name as the ping address:

```
/ # ping -c 2 ex
PING ex (172.17.0.3): 56 data bytes
64 bytes from 172.17.0.3: seq=0 ttl=64 time=0.108 ms
64 bytes from 172.17.0.3: seq=1 ttl=64 time=0.079 ms

--- ex ping statistics ---
2 packets transmitted, 2 packets received, 0% packet loss
round-trip min/avg/max = 0.079/0.093/0.108 ms
```

Evidently, the source container's alias `ex` is resolved to the IP address `172.17.0.3`, and the recipient container is able to successfully reach the source. In the case of secured container communication, pinging between containers is not allowed. We have given more details on the aspect of securing containers in *Chapter 11, Securing Docker Containers*.

In the preceding example, we could link two containers together, and also, observe how elegantly, networking is enabled between the containers by updating the source container's IP address in the `/etc/hosts` file of the recipient container.

The next example is to demonstrate how container-linking exports the source container's environment variables, which are configured using the `-e` option of the `docker run` subcommand or the `ENV` instruction of `Dockerfile`, to the recipient container. For this purpose, we are going to craft a `Dockerfile` with the `ENV` instruction, build an image, launch a source container using this image, and then launch a recipient container by linking it to the source container:

1. We begin with composing a `Dockerfile` with the `ENV` instruction, as shown here:

```
FROM busybox:latest
ENV BOOK="Learning Docker" \
    CHAPTER="Orchestrating Containers"
```

Here, we are setting up two environment variables `BOOK` and `CHAPTER`.

2. Proceed with building a Docker image `envex` using the `docker build` subcommand from the preceding `Dockerfile`:

```
$ sudo docker build -t envex .
```

3. Now, let's launch an interactive source container with the name `example` using the `envex` image, we just built:

```
$ sudo docker run -it --rm \
                --name example envex
```

4. From the source container prompt, display all the environment variables by invoking the `env` command:

```
/ # env
HOSTNAME=b53bc036725c
SHLVL=1
HOME=/root
TERM=xterm
PATH=/usr/local/sbin:/usr/local/bin:/usr/sbin:/usr/bin:/sbin:/
bin
BOOK=Learning Docker
CHAPTER=Orchestrating Containers
PWD=/
```

In all the preceding environment variables, both the BOOK and the CHAPTER variables are configured with the ENV instruction of the `Dockerfile`.

5. As a final step, to illustrate the ENV category of environment variables, launch the recipient container with the `env` command, as shown here:

```
$ sudo docker run --rm --link example:ex \
                busybox:latest env
PATH=/usr/local/sbin:/usr/local/bin:/usr/sbin:/usr/bin:/sbin:/
bin
HOSTNAME=a5e0c07fd643
TERM=xterm
EX_NAME=/stoic_hawking/ex
EX_ENV_BOOK=Learning Docker
EX_ENV_CHAPTER=Orchestrating Containers
HOME=/root
```

This example is also available on GitHub at `https://github.com/thedocker/learning-docker/blob/master/chap08/Dockerfile-Env`.

Strikingly, in the preceding output, the variables that are prefixed with `EX_` are the outcomes of container-linking. The environment variables of interest are `EX_ENV_BOOK` and `EX_ENV_CHAPTER`, which were originally set through the `Dockerfile` as `BOOK` and `CHAPTER` but modified to `EX_ENV_BOOK` and `EX_ENV_CHAPTER`, as an effect of container-linking. Though the environment variable names get translated, the values stored in these environment variables are preserved as is. We already discussed the `EX_NAME` variable name in the previous example.

In the preceding example, we could experience how elegantly and effortlessly Docker exports the `ENV` category variables from the source container to the recipient container. These environment variables are completely decoupled from the source and the recipient, thus the change in the value of these environment variables in one container does not impact the other. To be even more precise, the values the recipient container receives are the values set during the launch time of the source container. Any changes made to the value of these environment variables in the source container after its launch has no effect on the recipient container. It does not matter when the recipient container is launched because the values are being read from the JSON file.

In our final illustration of linking containers, we are going to show you how to take advantage of the Docker feature to share the connectivity details between two containers. In order to share the connectivity details between containers, Docker uses the `PORT` category of environment variables. The following are the steps used to craft two containers and share the connectivity details between them:

1. Craft a `Dockerfile` to expose port `80` and `8080` using the `EXPOSE` instruction, as shown here:

   ```
   FROM busybox:latest
   EXPOSE 8080 80
   ```

2. Proceed to build a Docker image `portex` using the `docker build` subcommand from the `Dockerfile`, we created just now, by running the following command:

   ```
   $ sudo docker build -t portex .
   ```

3. Now, let's launch an interactive source container with the name, example using the earlier built image portex:

```
$ sudo docker run -it --rm \
                    --name example portex
```

4. Now that we have launched the source container, let's continue to create a recipient container on another terminal by linking it to the source container, and invoke the env command to display all the environment variables, as shown here:

```
$ sudo docker run --rm --link example:ex \
                    busybox:latest env
PATH=/usr/local/sbin:/usr/local/bin:/usr/sbin:/usr/bin:/sbin:/
bin
HOSTNAME=c378bb55e69c
TERM=xterm
EX_PORT=tcp://172.17.0.4:80
EX_PORT_80_TCP=tcp://172.17.0.4:80
EX_PORT_80_TCP_ADDR=172.17.0.4
EX_PORT_80_TCP_PORT=80
EX_PORT_80_TCP_PROTO=tcp
EX_PORT_8080_TCP=tcp://172.17.0.4:8080
EX_PORT_8080_TCP_ADDR=172.17.0.4
EX_PORT_8080_TCP_PORT=8080
EX_PORT_8080_TCP_PROTO=tcp
EX_NAME=/prickly_rosalind/ex
HOME=/root
```

 This example is also available on GitHub at https://github.com/thedocker/learning-docker/blob/master/chap08/Dockerfile-Expose.

From the preceding output of the env command, it is quite evident that, the Docker engine exported a bunch of four PORT category environment variables for each port that was exposed using the EXPOSE instruction in the Dockerfile. In addition, Docker also exported another PORT category variable EX_PORT.

Orchestration of containers

The pioneering concept of orchestration in the IT domain has been there for a long time now. For instance, in the **service computing** (**SC**) arena, the idea of service orchestration has been thriving in an unprecedented manner in order to produce and sustain highly robust and resilient services. Discrete or atomic services do not serve any substantial purpose unless, they are composed together in a particular sequence to derive process-aware composite services. As orchestrated services are more strategically advantageous for businesses in expressing and exposing their unique capabilities in the form of identifiable/discoverable, interoperable, usable, and composable services to the outside world; corporates are showing exemplary interest in having an easily searchable repository of services (atomic as well as composite). This repository, in turn, enables businesses in realizing large-scale data as well as process-intensive applications. It is clear that the multiplicity of services is very pivotal for organizations to grow and glow. This increasingly mandated requirement gets solved using the proven and promising orchestration capabilities, cognitively.

Now, as we are fast heading toward containerized IT environments; application and data containers ought to be smartly composed to realize a host of new generation software services.

However, for producing highly competent orchestrated containers, both purpose-specific as well as agnostic containers need to be meticulously selected and launched in the right sequence in order to create orchestrated containers. The sequence can come from the process (control as well as data) flow diagrams. Doing this complicated and daunting activity manually evokes a series of cynicisms and criticisms. Fortunately, there are orchestration tools in the Docker space that come in handy to build, run, and manage multiple containers to build enterprise-class services. The Docker firm, which has been in charge of producing and promoting, the generation, and assembling of, Docker-inspired containers, has come out with a standardized and simplified orchestration tool (named as `docker-compose`) in order to reduce the workloads of developers as well as system administrators.

The proven composition technique of the service computing paradigm is being replicated here in the raging containerization paradigm in order to reap the originally envisaged benefits of containerization, especially in building powerful application-aware containers.

The **microservice architecture** is an architectural concept that aims to decouple a software solution by decomposing its functionality into a pool of discrete services. This is done by applying the standard principles at the architectural level. The microservice architecture is slowly emerging as a championed way to design and build large-scale IT and business systems. It not only facilitates loose and light coupling and software modularity, but it is also a boon to continuous integration and deployment for the agile world. Any changes being made to one part of the application mandate has meant, massive changes being made to the application. This has been a bane and barrier to the aspect of continuous deployment. Micro services aim to resolve this situation, and hence, the microservice architecture needs light-weight mechanisms, small, independently deployable services, and ensures scalability and portability. These requirements can be met using Docker-sponsored containers.

Micro services are being built around business capabilities and can be independently deployed by fully automated deployment machinery. Each micro service can be deployed without interrupting the other micro services, and containers provide an ideal deployment and execution environment for these services along with other noteworthy facilities, such as the reduced time of deployment, isolation management, and a simple life cycle. It is easy to quickly deploy new versions of services inside containers. All of these factors led to the explosion of micro services using the features that Docker had to offer.

As explained, Docker is being posited as the next-generation containerization technology, which provides a proven and potentially sound mechanism to distribute applications in a highly efficient and distributed fashion. The beauty is that developers can tweak the application pieces within the container, while maintaining the overall integrity of the container. This has a bigger impact as the brewing trend is that, instead of large monolithic applications hosted on a single physical or virtual server, companies are building smaller, self-defined, easily manageable, and discrete services to be contained inside standardized and automated containers. In short, the raging containerization technology from Docker has come as a boon for the ensuing era of micro services.

Docker was built and sustained to fulfill the elusive goal of *run it once and run it everywhere*. Docker containers are generally isolated at process level, portable across IT environments, and easily repeatable. A single physical host can host multiple containers, and hence, every IT environment is generally stuffed with a variety of Docker containers. The unprecedented growth of containers is to spell out troubles for effective container management. The multiplicity and the associated heterogeneity of containers are used to sharply increase the management complexities of containers. Hence, the technique of orchestration and the flourishing orchestration tools have come as a strategic solace for accelerating the containerization journey in safe waters.

Orchestrating applications that span multiple containers containing micro services has become a major part of the Docker world, via projects, such as Google's Kubernetes or Flocker. Decking is another option used to facilitate the orchestration of Docker containers. Docker's new offering in this area is a set of three orchestration services designed to cover all aspects of the dynamic life cycle of distributed applications from application development to deployment and maintenance. Helios is another Docker orchestration platform used to deploy and manage containers across an entire fleet. In the beginning, `fig` was the most preferred tool for container orchestration. However, in the recent past, the company at the forefront of elevating the Docker technology has come out with an advanced container orchestration tool (`docker-compose`) to make life easier for developers working with Docker containers, as they move through the container life cycle.

Having realized the significance of having the capability of container orchestration for next generation, business-critical, and containerized workloads, the Docker company purchased the company that originally conceived and concretized the `fig` tool. Then, the Docker company appropriately renamed the tool as `docker-compose` and brought in a good number of enhancements to make the tool more tuned to the varying expectations of container developers and operation teams.

Here is a gist of `docker-compose`, which is being positioned as a futuristic and flexible tool used for defining and running complex applications with Docker. With `docker-compose`, you define your application's components (their containers, configuration, links, volumes, and so on) in a single file, and then, you can spin everything up with a single command, which does everything to get it up and running.

This tool simplifies the container management by providing a set of built-in tools to do a number of jobs that are being performed manually at this point in time. In this section, we supply all the details for using `docker-compose` to perform orchestration of containers in order to have a stream of next-generation distributed applications.

Orchestrate containers using docker-compose

In this section, we will discuss the widely used container orchestration tool `docker-compose`. The `docker-compose` tool is a very simple, yet powerful tool and has been conceived and concretized to facilitate the running of a group of Docker containers. In other words, `docker-compose` is an orchestration framework that lets you define and control a multi-container service.

It enables you to create a fast and isolated development environment as well as the ability to orchestrate multiple Docker containers in production. The docker-compose tool internally leverages the Docker engine for pulling images, building the images, starting the containers in a correct sequence, and making the right connectivity/linking among the containers/services based on the definition given in the docker-compose.yml file.

Installing docker-compose

At the time of writing this book, the latest release of docker-compose is 1.2.0, and it is recommended that you use it with Docker release 1.3 or above. You can find the latest official release of docker-compose at the GitHub location (https://github.com/docker/compose/releases/latest).

The Linux x86-64 binary for docker-compose version 1.2.0 is available at https://github.com/docker/compose/releases/download/1.2.0/docker-compose-Linux-x86_64, which you can directly install using either the wget tool or the curl tool, as shown here:

- Using the wget tool:

```
$ sudo sh -c 'wget -qO-
https://github.com/docker/compose/releases/download/1.2.0/
docker-compose-'uname -s'-'uname -m' > /usr/local/bin/docker-
compose; chmod +x /usr/local/bin/docker-compose'
```

- Using the curl tool:

```
$ sudo sh -c 'curl  -sSL
https://github.com/docker/compose/releases/download/1.2.0/
docker-compose-'uname -s'-'uname -m' > /usr/local/bin/docker-
compose; chmod +x /usr/local/bin/docker-compose'
```

Alternatively, docker-compose is also available as a Python package, which you can install using the pip installer, as shown here:

```
$ sudo pip install -U docker-compose
```

 Note that if pip is not installed on the system, please install the pip package before the docker-compose installation.

Having successfully installed `docker-compose`, you can check the `docker-compose` version, as shown here:

```
$ docker-compose --version
docker-compose 1.2.0
```

The docker-compose.yml file

The `docker-compose` tool orchestrates containers using the `docker-compose.yml` file, in which you can define the services that need to be crafted, the relationships between these services, and their runtime properties. The `docker-compose.yml` file is a **YAML Ain't Markup Language (YAML)** format file, which is a human-friendly data serialization format. The default `docker-compose` file is `docker-compose.yml`, which can be changed using the `-f` option of the `docker-compose` tool. The following is the format of the `docker-compose.yml` file:

```
<service>:
    <key>: <value>
    <key>:
        - <value>
        - <value>
```

Here, `<service>` is the name of the service. You can have more than one service definition in a single `docker-compose.yml` file. The service name should be followed by one or more keys. However, all the services must either have an `image` or a `build` key, followed by any number of optional keys. Except the `image` and `build` keys, the rest of the keys can be directly mapped to the options in the `docker run` subcommand. The value can be either a single value or multiple values.

The following is a list of keys supported in the `docker-compose` version 1.2.0:

- `image`: This is the tag or image ID
- `build`: This is the path to a directory containing a `Dockerfile`
- `command`: This key overrides the default command
- `links`: This key links to containers in another service
- `external_links`: This key links to containers started either by some other `docker-compose.yml` or by some other means (not by `docker-compose`)

- `ports`: This key exposes ports and specifies both the ports `HOST_port:CONTAINER_port`
- `expose`: This key exposes ports without publishing them to the host machine
- `volumes`: This key mounts paths as volumes
- `volumes_from`: This key mounts all of the volumes from another container
- `environment`: This adds environment variables and uses either an array or a dictionary
- `env_file`: This adds environment variables to a file
- `extends`: This extends another service defined in the same or different configuration file
- `net`: This is the networking mode, which has the same values as the Docker client `--net` option
- `pid`: This enables the PID space sharing between the host and the containers
- `dns`: This sets custom DNS servers
- `cap_add`: This adds a capability to the container
- `cap_drop`: This drops a capability of the container
- `dns_search`: This sets custom DNS search servers
- `working_dir`: This changes the working directory inside the container
- `entrypoint`: This overrides the default entrypoint
- `user`: This sets the default user
- `hostname`: This sets a container's host name
- `domainname`: This sets the domain name

- `mem_limit`: This limits the memory
- `privileged`: This gives extended privileges
- `restart`: This sets the restart policy of the container
- `stdin_open`: This enables the standard input facility
- `tty`: This enables text based control such as a terminal
- `cpu_shares`: This sets the CPU shares (relative weight)

The docker-compose command

The `docker-compose` tool provides sophisticated orchestration functionality with a handful of commands. All the `docker-compose` commands use the `docker-compose.yml` file as the base to orchestrate one or more services. The following is the syntax of the `docker-compose` command:

```
docker-compose [<options>] <command> [<args>...]
```

The `docker-compose` tool supports the following options:

- `--verbose`: This shows more output
- `--version`: This prints the version and exits
- `-f, --file <file>`: This specifies an alternate file for `docker-compose` (default is the `docker-compose.yml` file)
- `-p, --project-name <name>`: This specifies an alternate project name (default is the directory name)

The `docker-compose` tool supports the following commands:

- `build`: This builds or rebuilds services
- `kill`: This kills containers
- `logs`: This displays the output from the containers
- `port`: This prints the public port for a port binding
- `ps`: This lists the containers
- `pull`: This pulls the service images
- `rm`: This removes the stopped containers
- `run`: This runs a one-off command
- `scale`: This sets a number of containers for a service
- `start`: This starts services
- `stop`: This stops services
- `up`: This creates and starts containers

Common usage

In this section, with the help of an example, we are going to experience the power of the orchestration feature provided by the Docker-Compose framework. For this purpose, we are going to build a two-tiered web application that will receive your inputs through a URL and respond back with the associated response text. This application is built using the following two services, as enumerated here:

- Redis: This is a key-value database used to store a key and its associated value
- Node.js: This is a JavaScript runtime environment used to implement web server functionality as well as the application logic

Each of these services is packed inside two different containers that are stitched together using the docker-compose tool. The following is the architectural representation of the services:

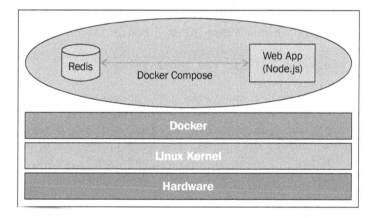

Here, in this example, we begin with implementing the example.js module, a node.js file to realize the web server and the key lookup functionality. Further on, we will craft the Dockerfile on the same directory as example.js to package the node.js runtime environment, and then, define the service orchestration using a docker-compose.yml file on the same directory as example.js.

The following is the `example.js` file, which is a `node.js` implementation of the simple Request/Response web application. For demonstration purposes, in this code, we restrict the `build` and `kill docker-compose` commands. For the code to be self-explanatory, we added the comments in between the code:

```
// A Simple Request/Response web application

// Load all required libraries
var http = require('http');
var url = require('url');
var redis = require('redis');

// Connect to redis server running
// createClient API is called with
//   -- 6379, a well-known port to which the
//            redis server listens to
//   -- redis, is the link name of the container
//             that runs redis server
var client = redis.createClient(6379, 'redis');

// Set the key value pair in the redis server

// Here all the keys proceeds with "/", because
// URL parser always have "/" as its first character
client.set("/", "Welcome to Docker-Compose helper\nEnter the
docker-compose command in the URL for help\n", redis.print);
client.set("/build", "Build or rebuild services", redis.print);
client.set("/kill", "Kill contianers", redis.print);

var server = http.createServer(function (request, response) {
  var href = url.parse(request.url, true).href;
  response.writeHead(200, {"Content-Type": "text/plain"});

  // Pull the response (value) string using the URL
  client.get(href, function (err, reply) {
    if ( reply == null ) response.write("Command: " +
href.slice(1) + " not supported\n");
    else response.write(reply + "\n");
    response.end();
  });
});

console.log("Listening on port 80");
server.listen(80);
```

This example is also available at https://github.com/
thedocker/learning-docker/tree/master/chap08/
orchestrate-using-compose.

The following text is the content of Dockerfile that packs the node.js image,
the redis driver for node.js, and the example.js file as defined earlier:

```
##############################################
# Dockerfile to build a sample web application
##############################################

# Base image is node.js
FROM node:latest

# Author: Dr. Peter
MAINTAINER Dr. Peter <peterindia@gmail.com>

# Install redis driver for node.js
RUN npm install redis

# Copy the source code to the Docker image
ADD example.js /myapp/example.js
```

This code is also available at https://github.com/
thedocker/learning-docker/tree/master/chap08/
orchestrate-using-compose.

The following text is from the docker-compose.yml file that the defines the service
orchestration for docker compose tool to act upon:

```
web:
  build: .
  command: node /myapp/example.js
  links:
   - redis
  ports:
   - 8080:80
redis:
  image: redis:latest
```

This example is also available at `https://github.com/
thedocker/learning-docker/tree/master/chap08/
orchestrate-using-compose`.

We defined two services in this `docker-compose.yml` file, wherein these services serve the following purposes:

- The service named `web` is built using the `Dockerfile` in the current directory. Also, it is instructed to launch the container by running the node (the `node.js` runtime) with `/myapp/example.js` (web application implementation), as its argument. The container is linked to the `redis` container, and the container port `80` is mapped to the Docker host's port `8080`.

- The service named `redis` is instructed to launch a container with the `redis:latest` image. If the image is not present in the Docker host, the Docker engine will pull it from the central repository or the private repository.

Now, let's continue with our example by building the Docker images using the `docker-compose build` command, launch the containers using the `docker-compose up` command, and connect with a browser to verify the request/response functionality, as explained step by step here:

1. The `docker-compose` commands must be executed from the directory in which the `docker-compose.yml` file is stored. The `docker-compose` tool considers each `docker-compose.yml` file as a project, and it assumes the project name from the `docker-compose.yml` file's directory. Of course, this can be overridden using the -p option. So, as a first step, let's change the directory, wherein the `docker-compose.yml` file is stored:

   ```
   $ cd ~/example
   ```

2. Build the services using the `docker-compose build` command:

   ```
   $ sudo docker-compose build
   ```

3. Proceed to bring up the services as indicated in the `docker-compose.yml`, file using the `docker-compose up` command:

   ```
   $ sudo docker-compose up
   Creating example_redis_1...
   Pulling image redis:latest...
   latest: Pulling from redis
   ```

```
21e4345e9035: Pull complete

. . . TRUNCATED OUTPUT . . .

redis:latest: The image you are pulling has been verified.

Important: image verification is a tech preview feature and
should not be relied on to provide security.

Digest: sha256:dad98e997480d657b2c00085883640c747b04ca882d6da50760
e038fce63e1b5

Status: Downloaded newer image for redis:latest

Creating example_web_1...

Attaching to example_redis_1, example_web_1

. . . TRUNCATED OUTPUT . . .

redis_1 | 1:M 25 Apr 18:12:59.674 * The server is now ready to
accept connections on port 6379

web_1   | Listening on port 80

web_1   | Reply: OK

web_1   | Reply: OK

web_1   | Reply: OK
```

Since the directory name is example, the docker-compose tool has assumed that the project name is example.

4. Having successfully orchestrated the services using the docker-compose tool, let's invoke the docker-compose ps command from a different terminal to list the containers associated with the example docker-compose project:

```
$ sudo docker-compose ps
      Name                    Command               State
Ports
-------------------------------------------------------------
-------------
example_redis_1    /entrypoint.sh redis-server    Up
6379/tcp
example_web_1      node /myapp/example.js         Up
0.0.0.0:8080->80/tcp
```

Evidently, the two example_redis_1 and example_web_1 containers are up and running. The container name is prefixed with example_, which is the docker-compose project name.

5. Explore the functionality of our own request/response web application on a different terminal of the Docker host, as illustrated here:

```
$ curl http://0.0.0.0:8080
Welcome to Docker-Compose helper
Enter the docker-compose command in the URL for help
$ curl http://0.0.0.0:8080/build
Build or rebuild services
$ curl http://0.0.0.0:8080/something
Command: something not supported
```

> Here, we are directly connecting to the web service using http://0.0.0.0:8080 because the web service is bound to the Docker host on port 8080.

Cool, isn't it? With very minimal effort, and the help of the docker-compose.yml file, we are able to compose two different services together and offer a composite service.

Summary

This chapter has been incorporated in the book in order to provide all the probing and prescribing details on seamlessly orchestrating multiple containers. We extensively discussed the need for container orchestration and the tools that enable us to simplify and streamline the increasingly complicated process of container orchestration. In order to substantiate how orchestration is handy and helpful in crafting enterprise-class containers, and to illustrate the orchestration process, we took the widely followed route of explaining the whole gamut through a simple example. We developed a web application and contained it within a standard container. Similarly, we took a database container, which is a backend for the frontend web application and the database was executed inside another container. We saw how to make the web application container aware of the database, using different technologies through the container-linkage feature of the Docker engine. We used the open source tool (docker-compose) for this purpose.

In the next chapter, we will discuss how Docker facilitates software testing, especially integration testing with a few pragmatic examples.

9
Testing with Docker

Undoubtedly, the trait of testing has been at the forefront of the software engineering discipline. It is widely accepted that there is a deep and decisive penetration of software into every kind of tangible object in our daily environments these days in order to have plenty of smart, connected, and digitized assets. Also, with a heightened focus on distributed and synchronized software, the complexity of the software design, development, testing and debugging, deployment, and delivery are continuously on the climb. There are means and mechanisms being unearthed to simplify and streamline the much-needed automation of software building and the authentication of software reliability, resiliency, and sustainability. Docker is emerging as an extremely flexible tool to test a wide variety of software applications. In this chapter, we are going to discuss how to effectively leverage the noteworthy Docker advancements for software testing and its unique advantages in accelerating and augmenting testing automation.

The following topics are discussed in this chapter:

- A brief overview of **test-driven development** (TDD)
- Testing your code inside Docker
- Integrating the Docker testing process into Jenkins

The emerging situation is that Docker containers are being leveraged to create development and testing environments that are the exact replicas of the production environment. Containers require less overhead when compared to virtual machines, which have been the primary environments for development, staging, and deployment environments. Let's start with an overview of test-driven development of the next generation software and how the Docker-inspired containerization becomes handy in simplifying the TDD process.

A brief overview of the test-driven development

The long and arduous journey of software development has taken many turns and twists in the past decades, and one of the prominent software engineering techniques is nonetheless the TDD. There are more details and documents on TDD at `http://agiledata.org/essays/tdd.html`.

In a nutshell, the test-driven development, also popularly known as TDD, is a software development practice in which the development cycle begins with writing a test case that would fail, then writes the actual software to make the test pass, and continues to refactor and repeat the cycle till the software reaches the acceptable level. This process is depicted in the following diagram:

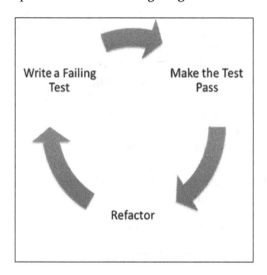

Testing your code inside Docker

In this section, we will take you through a journey in which we will show you how TDD is done using stubs, and how Docker can come handy in developing software in the deployment equivalent system. For this purpose, we take a web application use case that has a feature to track the visit count of each of its users. For this example, we use Python as the implementation language and `redis` as the key-value pair database to store the users hit count. Besides, to showcase the testing capability of Docker, we limit our implementation to just two functions: `hit` and `getHit`.

NOTE: All the examples in this chapter use `python3` as the runtime environment. The `ubuntu 14.04` installation comes with `python3` by default. If you don't have `python3` installed on your system, refer to the respective manual to install `python3`.

As per the TDD practice, we start by adding unit test cases for the `hit` and `getHit` functionalities, as depicted in the following code snippet. Here, the test file is named `test_hitcount.py`:

```python
import unittest
import hitcount

class HitCountTest (unittest.TestCase):
    def testOneHit(self):
        # increase the hit count for user user1
        hitcount.hit("user1")
        # ensure that the hit count for user1 is just 1
        self.assertEqual(b'1', hitcount.getHit("user1"))

if __name__ == '__main__':
    unittest.main()
```

This example is also available at `https://github.com/thedocker/testing/tree/master/src`.

Here, in the first line, we are importing the `unittest` Python module that provides the necessary framework and functionality to run the unit test and generate a detailed report on the test execution. In the second line, we are importing the `hitcount` Python module, where we are going to implement the hit count functionality. Then, we will continue to add the test code that would test the `hitcount` module's functionality.

Now, run the test suite using the unit test framework of Python, as follows:

```
$ python3 -m unittest
```

The following is the output generated by the unit test framework:

```
E
========================================================================
ERROR: test_hitcount (unittest.loader.ModuleImportFailure)
------------------------------------------------------------------------
Traceback (most recent call last):
...OUTPUT TRUNCATED ...
ImportError: No module named 'hitcount'



------------------------------------------------------------------------
Ran 1 test in 0.001s

FAILED (errors=1)
```

As expected, the test failed with the error message `ImportError: No module named 'hitcount'` because we had not even created the file and hence, it could not import the `hitcount` module.

Now, create a file with the name `hitcount.py` in the same directory as `test_hitcount.py`:

```
$ touch hitcount.py
```

Continue to run the unit test suite:

```
$ python3 -m unittest
```

The following is the output generated by the unit test framework:

```
E
========================================================================
ERROR: testOneHit (test_hitcount.HitCountTest)
------------------------------------------------------------------------
Traceback (most recent call last):
  File "/home/user/test_hitcount.py", line 10, in testOneHit
    hitcount.hit("peter")
```

```
AttributeError: 'module' object has no attribute 'hit'
```

```
----------------------------------------------------------------
```

```
Ran 1 test in 0.001s
```

```
FAILED (errors=1)
```

Again the test suite failed like the earlier but with a different error message `AttributeError: 'module' object has no attribute 'hit'`. We are getting this error because we have not implemented the `hit` function yet.

Let's proceed to implement the `hit` and `getHit` functions in `hitcount.py`, as shown here:

```
import redis
# connect to redis server
r = redis.StrictRedis(host='0.0.0.0', port=6379, db=0)

# increase the hit count for the usr
def hit(usr):
    r.incr(usr)

# get the hit count for the usr
    def getHit(usr):
        return (r.get(usr))
```

This example is also available on GitHub at `https://github.com/thedocker/testing/tree/master/src`.

Note: To continue with this example, you must have the python3 compatible version of package installer (pip3).

The following command is used to install pip3:

```
$ wget -qO- https://bootstrap.pypa.io/get-pip.py |
sudo python3 -
```

In the first line of this program, we are importing the `redis` driver, which is the connectivity driver of the `redis` database. In the following line, we are connecting to the `redis` database, and then we will continue to implement the `hit` and `getHit` function.

The `redis` driver is an optional Python module, so let's proceed to install the `redis` driver using the pip installer, which is illustrated as follows:

```
$ sudo pip3 install redis
```

Our `unittest` will still fail even after installing the `redis` driver because we are not running a `redis` database server yet. So, we can either run a `redis` database server to successfully complete our unit testing or take the traditional TDD approach of mocking the `redis` driver. Mocking is a testing approach wherein complex behavior is substituted by predefined or simulated behavior. In our example, to mock the redis driver, we are going to leverage a third-party Python package called mockredis. This mock package is available at `https://github.com/locationlabs/mockredis` and the `pip` installer name is `mockredispy`. Let's install this mock using the pip installer:

```
$ sudo pip3 install mockredispy
```

Having installed `mockredispy`, the `redis` mock, let's refactor our test code `test_hitcount.py` (which we had written earlier) to use the simulated `redis` functionality provided by the `mockredis` module. This is accomplished by the patch method provided by the `unittest.mock` mocking framework, as shown in the following code:

```python
import unittest
from unittest.mock import patch

# Mock for redis
import mockredis
import hitcount

class HitCountTest(unittest.TestCase):


    @patch('hitcount.r',mockredis.mock_strict_redis_client(host='0.0.0.0',
    port=6379,
    db=0))
        def testOneHit(self):
            # increase the hit count for user user1
            hitcount.hit("user1")
            # ensure that the hit count for user1 is just 1
            self.assertEqual(b'1', hitcount.getHit("user1"))

    if __name__ == '__main__':
        unittest.main()
```

This example is also available on GitHub at `https://github.com/thedocker/testing/tree/master/src`.

Now, run the test suite again:

```
$ python3 -m unittest
.
----------------------------------------------------------------------
-

Ran 1 test in 0.000s

OK
```

Finally, as we can see in the preceding output, we successfully implemented our visitors count functionality through the test, code, and refactor cycle.

Running the test inside a container

In the previous section, we walked you through the complete cycle of TDD, in which we installed additional Python packages to complete our development. However, in the real world, one might work on multiple projects that might have conflicting libraries and hence, there is a need for the isolation of runtime environments. Before the advent of Docker technology, the Python community used to leverage the `virtualenv` tool to isolate the Python runtime environment. Docker takes this isolation a step further by packaging the OS, the Python tool chain, and the runtime environment. This type of isolation gives a lot of flexibility to the development community to use appropriate software versions and libraries as per the project needs.

Here is the step-by-step procedure to package the test and visitor count implementation of the previous section to a Docker container and perform the test inside the container:

1. Craft a `Dockerfile` to build an image with the `python3` runtime, the `redis` and `mockredispy` packages, both the `test_hitcount.py` test file and the visitors count implementation `hitcount.py`, and finally, launch the unit test:

```
###############################################
# Dockerfile to build the unittest container
###############################################
```

```
# Base image is python
FROM python:latest

# Author: Dr. Peter
MAINTAINER Dr. Peter <peterindia@gmail.com>

# Install redis driver for python and the redis mock
RUN pip install redis && pip install mockredispy

# Copy the test and source to the Docker image
ADD src/ /src/

# Change the working directory to /src/
WORKDIR /src/

# Make unittest as the default execution
ENTRYPOINT python3 -m unittest
```

 This example is also available on GitHub at `https://github.com/thedocker/testing/tree/master/src`.

2. Now create a directory called `src` on the directory, where we crafted our `Dockerfile`. Move the `test_hitcount.py` and `hitcount.py` files to the newly created `src` directory.

3. Build the `hit_unittest` Docker image using the `docker build` subcommand:

```
$ sudo docker build -t hit_unittest .
Sending build context to Docker daemon 11.78 kB
Sending build context to Docker daemon
Step 0 : FROM python:latest
 ---> 32b9d937b993
Step 1 : MAINTAINER Dr. Peter <peterindia@gmail.com>
 ---> Using cache
 ---> bf40ee5f5563
Step 2 : RUN pip install redis && pip install mockredispy
 ---> Using cache
 ---> a55f3bdb62b3
```

```
Step 3 : ADD src/ /src/
 ---> 526e13dbf4c3
Removing intermediate container a6d89cbce053
Step 4 : WORKDIR /src/
 ---> Running in 5c180e180a93
 ---> 53d3f4e68f6b
Removing intermediate container 5c180e180a93
Step 5 : ENTRYPOINT python3 -m unittest
 ---> Running in 74d81f4fe817
 ---> 063bfe92eae0
Removing intermediate container 74d81f4fe817
Successfully built 063bfe92eae0
```

4. Now that we have successfully built the image, let's launch our container with the unit testing bundle using the `docker run` subcommand, as illustrated here:

```
$ sudo docker run --rm -it hit_unittest .
----------------------------------------------------------------
----
Ran 1 test in 0.001s
```

OK

Apparently, the unit test ran successfully with no errors because we already packaged the tested code.

In this approach, for every change, the Docker image is built and then, the container is launched to complete the test.

Using a Docker container as a runtime environment

In the previous section, we built a Docker image to perform the testing. Particularly, in the TDD practice, the unit test cases and the code go through multiple changes. Consequently, the Docker image needs to be built over and over again, which is a daunting job. In this section, we will see an alternative approach in which the Docker container is built with a runtime environment, the development directory is mounted as a volume, and the test is performed inside the container.

During this TDD cycle, if an additional library or update to the existing library is required, then the container will be updated with the required libraries and the updated container will be committed as a new image. This approach gives the isolation and flexibility that any developer would dream of because the runtime and its dependency live within the container, and any misconfigured runtime environment can be discarded and a new runtime environment can be built from a previously working image. This also helps to preserve the sanity of the Docker host from the installation and uninstallation of libraries.

The following example is a step-by-step instruction on how to use the Docker container as a nonpolluting yet very powerful runtime environment:

1. We begin with launching the Python runtime interactive container, using the `docker run` subcommand:

   ```
   $ sudo docker run -it \
               -v /home/peter/src/hitcount:/src \
               python:latest /bin/bash
   ```

   Here, in this example, the `/home/peter/src/hitcount` Docker host directory is earmarked as the placeholder for the source code and test files. This directory is mounted in the container as `/src`.

2. Now, on another terminal of the Docker host, copy both the `test_hitcount.py` test file and the visitors count implementation `hitcount.py` to `/home/peter/src/hitcount` directory.

3. Switch to the Python runtime interactive container terminal, change the current working directory to `/src`, and run the unit test:

   ```
   root@a8219ac7ed8e:~# cd /src
   root@a8219ac7ed8e:/src# python3 -m unittest
   E
   ======================================================================
   ====
   ERROR: test_hitcount (unittest.loader.ModuleImportFailure)
   . . . TRUNCATED OUTPUT . . .
     File "/src/test_hitcount.py", line 4, in <module>
       import mockredis
   ImportError: No module named 'mockredis'


   ----------------------------------------------------------------------
   ```

```
Ran 1 test in 0.001s
```

```
FAILED (errors=1)
```

Evidently, the test failed because it could not find the `mockredis` Python library.

4. Proceed to install the `mockredispy` pip package because the previous step failed, as it could not find the `mockredis` library in the runtime environment:

```
root@a8219ac7ed8e:/src# pip install mockredispy
```

5. Rerun the Python unit test:

```
root@a8219ac7ed8e:/src# python3 -m unittest
E
======================================================================
ERROR: test_hitcount (unittest.loader.ModuleImportFailure)
. . . TRUNCATED OUTPUT . . .
  File "/src/hitcount.py", line 1, in <module>
    import redis
ImportError: No module named 'redis'
```

```
Ran 1 test in 0.001s
```

```
FAILED (errors=1)
```

Again, the test failed because the `redis` driver is not yet installed.

6. Continue to install the `redis` driver using the pip installer, as shown here:

```
root@a8219ac7ed8e:/src# pip install redis
```

7. Having successfully installed the `redis` driver, let's once again run the unit test:

```
root@a8219ac7ed8e:/src# python3 -m unittest
.
----------------------------------------------------------------------
Ran 1 test in 0.000s
```

```
OK
```

Apparently, this time the unit test passed with no warnings or error messages.

8. Now we have a runtime environment that is good enough to run our test cases. It is better to commit these changes to a Docker image for reuse, using the `docker commit` subcommand:

```
$ sudo docker commit a8219ac7ed8e python_rediswithmock
fcf27247ff5bb240a935ec4ba1bddbd8c90cd79cba66e52b21e1b48f984c7db2
```

From now on, we can use the `python_rediswithmock` image to launch new containers for our TDD.

In this section, we vividly illustrated the approach on how to use the Docker container as a testing environment, and also at the same time, preserve the sanity and sanctity of the Docker host by isolating and limiting the runtime dependency within the container.

Integrating Docker testing into Jenkins

In the previous section, we laid out a stimulating foundation on software testing, how to leverage the Docker technology for the software testing, and the unique benefits of the container technology during the testing phase. In this section, we will introduce you to the steps required to prepare the Jenkins environment for testing with Docker, and then, demonstrate how Jenkins can be extended to integrate and automate testing with Docker using the well-known hit count use case.

Preparing the Jenkins environment

In this section, we will take you through the steps to install `jenkins`, GitHub plugin for Jenkins and `git`, and the revision control tool. These steps are as follows:

1. We begin with adding the Jenkins' trusted PGP public key:

```
$ wget -q -O - \
    https://jenkins-ci.org/debian/jenkins-ci.org.key | \
    sudo apt-key add -
```

Here, we are using `wget` to download the PGP public key, and then we add it to the list of trusted keys using the apt-key tool. Since Ubuntu and Debian share the same software packaging, Jenkins provides a single common package for both Ubuntu and Debian.

2. Add the Debian package location to the `apt` package source list, as follows:

```
$ sudo sh -c \
   'echo deb http://pkg.jenkins-ci.org/debian binary/ > \
   /etc/apt/sources.list.d/jenkins.list'
```

3. Having added the package source, continue to run the `apt-get` command update option to resynchronize the package index from the sources:

```
$ sudo apt-get update
```

4. Now, install `jenkins` using the `apt-get` command install option, as demonstrated here:

```
$ sudo apt-get install jenkins
```

5. Finally, activate the `jenkins` service using the `service` command:

```
$ sudo service jenkins start
```

6. The `jenkins` service can be accessed through any web browsers by specifying the IP address (`10.1.1.13`) of the system in which Jenkins is installed. The default port number for Jenkins is `8080`. The following screenshot is the entry page or **Dashboard** of **Jenkins**:

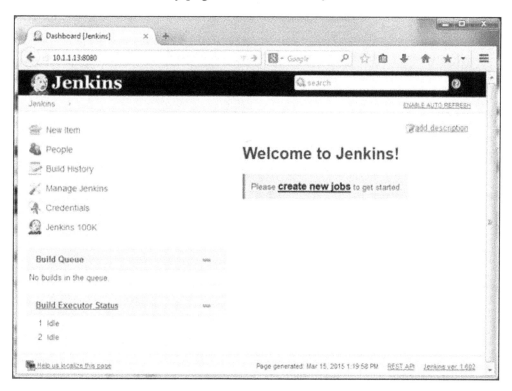

7. In this example, we are going to use GitHub as the source code repository. Jenkins does not support GitHub by default and hence, we need to install the GitHub plugin. During the installation, sometimes Jenkins does not populate the plugin availability list, and hence, you have to force it to download the list of available plugins. You can do so by performing the following steps:

1. Select **Manage Jenkins** on the left-hand side of the screen, which will take us to a **Manage Jenkins** page, as shown in the following screenshot:

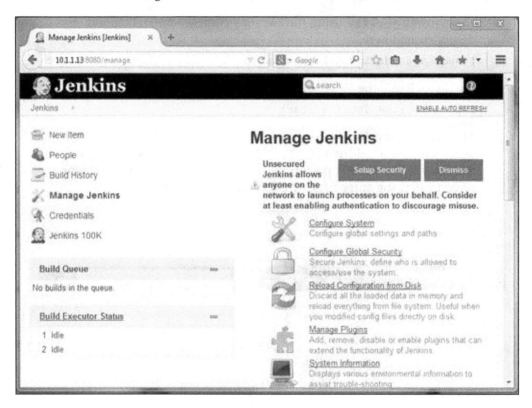

2. On the **Manage Jenkins** page, select **Manage Plugins** and this will take us to the **Plugin Manager** page, as shown in the following screenshot:

3. Here, on the **Plugin Manager** page, select the **Advanced** tab, go to the bottom of this page, and you will find the **Check now** button in the right-hand side corner of the page. Click on the **Check now** button to start the plugin updates. Alternatively, you can directly go to the **Check now** button on the **Advanced** page by navigating to `http://<jenkins-server>:8080/pluginManager/advanced`, wherein `<jenkins-server>` is the IP address of the system in which Jenkins is installed.

 NOTE: If Jenkins does not update the available plugin list, it is most likely a mirror site issue, so modify the **Update Site** field with a working mirror URL.

8. Having updated the available plugin list, let's continue to install the GitHub plugin, as depicted in the following substeps:

    1. Select the **Available** tab in the **Plugin Manager** page, which will list all the available plugins.

    2. Type GitHub plugin as the filter, which will list just the GitHub plugin, as shown in the following screenshot:

    3. Select the checkbox, and click on **Download now and install after restart**. You will be taken to a screen that will show you the progress of the plugin installation:

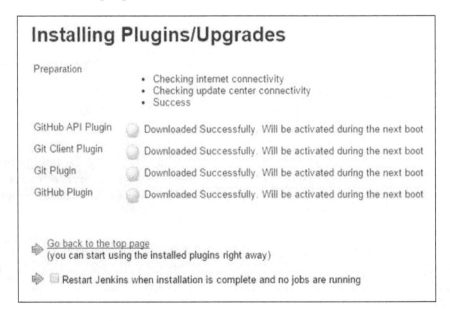

4. After all the plugins have successfully downloaded, go ahead and restart Jenkins using `http://< jenkins-server >:8080/restart`, where `<jenkins-server>` is the IP address of the system in which Jenkins is installed.

9. Ensure that the `git` package is installed, otherwise install the `git` package using the `apt-get` command:

```
$ sudo apt-get install git
```

10. So far, we have been running the Docker client using the `sudo` command, but unfortunately, we could not invoke `sudo` inside Jenkins because sometimes it prompts for a password. To overcome the `sudo` password prompt issue, we can make use of the Docker group, wherein any user who is part of the Docker group can invoke the Docker client without using the `sudo` command. Jenkins installation always sets up a user and group called `jenkins` and runs the Jenkins server using that user and group. So, we just need to add the `jenkins` user to the Docker group to get the Docker client working without the `sudo` command:

```
$ sudo gpasswd -a jenkins docker

Adding user jenkins to group docker
```

11. Restart the `jenkins` service for the group change to take effect using the following command:

```
$ sudo service jenkins restart

 * Restarting Jenkins Continuous Integration Server jenkins
[ OK ]
```

We have set up a Jenkins environment that is now capable of automatically pulling the latest source code from the `http://github.com` repository, packaging it as a Docker image, and executing the prescribed test scenarios.

Automating the Docker testing process

In this section, we will explore how to automate testing using Jenkins and Docker. As mentioned earlier, we are going to use GitHub as our repository. We have already uploaded the `Dockerfile`, `test_hitcount.py`, and `hitcount.py` files of our previous example to GitHub at `https://github.com/thedocker/testing`, which we are to use in the ensuing example. However, we strongly encourage you to set up your own repository at `http://github.com`, using the fork option that you can find at `https://github.com/thedocker/testing`, and substitute this address wherever applicable in the ensuing example.

The following are the detailed steps to automate the Docker testing:

1. Configure Jenkins to trigger a build when a file is modified in the GitHub repository, which is illustrated in the following substeps:

   1. Connect to the Jenkins server again.

   2. Select either **New Item** or **create new jobs**:

   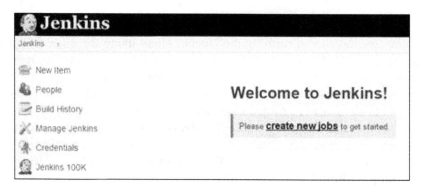

   3. In the following screenshot, give a name to the project (for example, Docker-Testing), and select the **Freestyle project** radio button:

   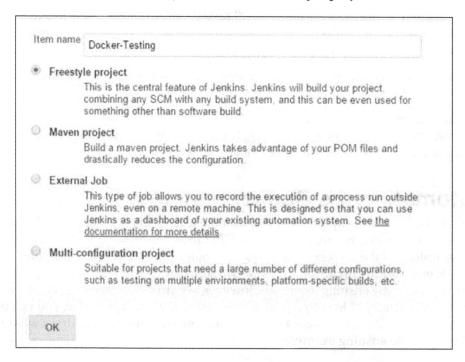

4. In the next screenshot, select the **Git** radio button under **Source Code Management**, and specify the GitHub repository URL in the **Repository URL** text field:

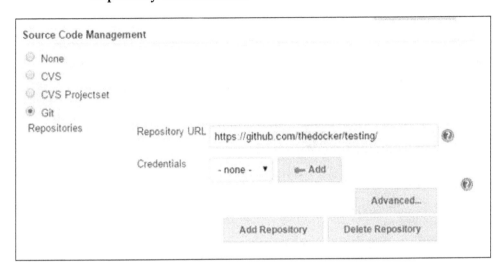

5. Select **Poll SCM** under **Build Triggers** to schedule GitHub polling for every 15 minute interval. Type the following line of code H/15 * * * * in the **Schedule** textbox, as shown in the following screenshot. For testing purposes, you can reduce the polling interval:

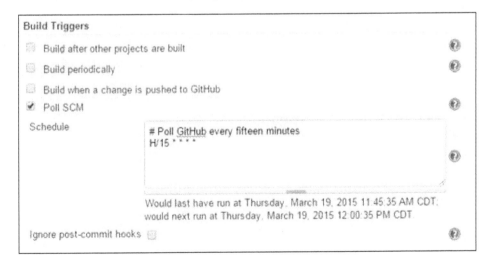

6. Scroll down the screen a little further, and select the **Add build step** button under **Build**. In the drop-down list, select **Execute shell** and type in the text, as shown in the following screenshot:

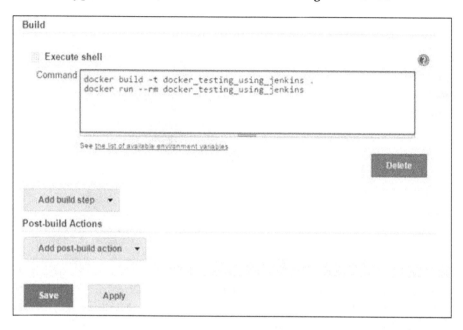

7. Finally, save the configuration by clicking on the **Save** button.

2. Go back to the Jenkins Dashboard, and you can find your test listed on the dashboard:

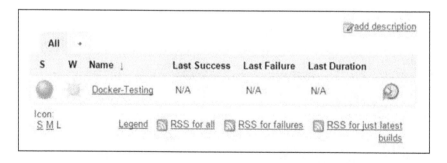

3. You can either wait for the Jenkins schedule to kick-start the build, or you can click on the clock icon on the right-hand side of the screen to kick-start the build immediately. As soon as the build is done, the Dashboard is updated with the build status as a success or failure, and the build number:

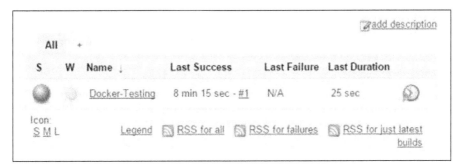

4. If you hover the mouse closer to the build number, you will get a drop-down button with options, such as **Changes**, **Console Output**, and so on, as shown in the following screenshot:

5. The **Console Output** option will show the details highlighted for the build, as follows:

```
Started by user anonymous
Building in workspace /var/lib/jenkins/jobs/Docker-Testing/
workspace
Cloning the remote Git repository
Cloning repository https://github.com/thedocker/testing/
. . . OUTPUT TRUNCATED . . .
+ docker build -t docker_testing_using_jenkins .
Sending build context to Docker daemon 121.9 kB

Sending build context to Docker daemon
Step 0 : FROM python:latest
. . . OUTPUT TRUNCATED . . .
Successfully built ad4be4b451e6
+ docker run --rm docker_testing_using_jenkins
  .
------------------------------------------------------------------
----
Ran 1 test in 0.000s

OK
Finished: SUCCESS
```

6. Evidently, the test failed because of the wrong module name **error_hitcount**, which we deliberately introduced. Now, let's experiment a negative scenario by deliberately introducing a bug in **test_hitcount.py** and observe the effect the on Jenkins build. As we have configured Jenkins, it faithfully polls the GitHub and kick-starts the build:

Apparently, the build failed as we expected.

7. As a final step, open **Console Output** of the failed build:

```
Started by an SCM change
Building in workspace /var/lib/jenkins/jobs/Docker-Testing/
workspace
. . . OUTPUT TRUNCATED . . .
ImportError: No module named 'error_hitcount'


--------------------------------------------------------------------
----
Ran 1 test in 0.001s


FAILED (errors=1)
Build step 'Execute shell' marked build as failure
Finished: FAILURE
```

Evidently, the test failed because of the wrong module name
error_hitcount, which we deliberately introduced.

Cool, isn't it? We automated our testing using Jenkins and Docker. Besides, we are
able to experience the power of testing automation using Jenkins and Docker. In a
large-scale project, Jenkins and Docker can be combined together to automate the
complete unit testing needs, and thus, to automatically capture any defects and
deficiencies introduced by any developers.

Summary

The potential benefits of containerization are being discovered across the breadth
and the length of software engineering. Previously, testing sophisticated software
systems involved a number of expensive and hard-to-manage server modules and
clusters. Considering the costs and complexities involved, most of the software
testing is accomplished using mocking procedures and stubs. All of this is going
to end for good with the maturity of the Docker technology. The openness and
flexibility of Docker enables it to work seamlessly with other technologies to
substantially reduce the testing time and complexity.

For a long time, the leading ways of testing software systems included mocking, dependency, injection, and so on. Usually, these mandate creating many sophisticated abstractions in the code. The current practice for developing and running test cases against an application is actually done on stubs rather than on the full application. That is, with a containerized workflow, it is very much possible to test against real application containers with all the dependencies. The contributions of the Docker paradigm, especially for the testing phenomenon and phase are therefore being carefully expounded and recorded in the recent past. Precisely speaking, the field of software engineering is moving towards smart and sunnier days with all the innovations in the Docker space.

In this chapter, we clearly expounded and explained a powerful testing framework for integrated applications using the Docker-inspired containerization paradigm. Increasingly for the agile world, the proven and potential TDD method is being insisted as an efficient software building and sustenance methodology. This chapter has utilized the Python unit test framework to illustrate how the TDD methodology is a pioneering tool for software engineering. The unit test framework is tweaked to be efficiently and elegantly containerized, and the Docker container is seamlessly integrated with Jenkins, which is a modern day deployment tool for continuous delivery, and is part and parcel of the agile programming world, as described in this chapter. The Docker container source code is pre-checked before it enters into the GitHub code repository. The Jenkins tool downloads the code from GitHub and runs the test inside a container. In the next chapter, we shall will dive deep into, and describe the theoretical aspects of, the process isolation through the container technology and various debugging tools and techniques.

10
Debugging Containers

Debugging has been an artistic component in the field of software engineering. All kinds of software building blocks individually, as well as collectively, need to go through a stream of deeper and decisive investigations by software development and testing professionals in order to ensure the security and safety of the resulting software applications. As Docker containers are said to be key runtime environments for next generation mission-critical software workloads, it is pertinent and paramount for containers, crafters, and composers to embark on the systematic and sagacious verification and validation of containers.

This chapter has been dedicatedly written to enable technical guys with all the right and relevant information to meticulously debug applications running inside containers and containers themselves. In this chapter, we will take a look at the theoretical aspects of process isolation for processes running as containers. A Docker container runs at a user-level process on host machines and typically has the same isolation level as provided by the operating system. With the release of Docker 1.5, many debugging tools are available, which can be efficiently used to debug your applications. We will also cover the primary Docker debugging tools, such as Docker exec, stats, ps, top, events, and logs. Finally, we will take a look at the nsenter tool to log in to containers without running the **Secure Shell** (**SSH**) daemon.

The list of topics that will be covered in the chapter is as follows:

- Process level isolation for Docker containers
- Debugging a containerized application
- Installing and using nsenter

Process level isolation for Docker containers

In the virtualization paradigm, the hypervisor emulates computing resources and provides a virtualized environment called a VM to install the operating system and applications on top of it. Whereas, in the case of the container paradigm, a single system (bare metal or virtual machine) is effectively partitioned to run multiple services simultaneously without interfering with each other. These services must be isolated from each other in order to prevent them from stepping on each other's resources or dependency conflict (also known as dependency hell). The Docker container technology essentially achieves process-level isolation by leveraging the Linux kernel constructs, such as namespaces and cgroups, particularly, the namespaces. The Linux kernel provides the following five powerful namespace leavers to isolate the global system resources from each other. These are the **Interprocess Communication** (**IPC**) namespaces used to isolate the interprocess communication resources:

- The network namespace is used to isolate networking resources, such as the network devices, network stack, port number, and so on
- The mount namespace isolates the filesystem mount points
- The PID namespace isolates the process identification number
- The user namespace is used to isolate the user ID and group ID
- The UTS namespace is used to isolate the hostname and the NIS domain name

These namespaces add an additional level of complexity when we have to debug the services running inside the containers, which we will learn more in detail in the next chapter.

In this section, we will discuss how the Docker engine provides process isolation by leveraging the Linux namespaces through a series of practical examples, and one of them is listed here:

1. Start by launching an `ubuntu` container in an interactive mode using the `docker run` subcommand, as shown here:

   ```
   $ sudo docker run -it --rm ubuntu /bin/bash
   root@93f5d72c2f21:/#
   ```

2. Proceed to find the process ID of the preceding container `93f5d72c2f21`, using the `docker inspect` subcommand in a different terminal:

```
$ sudo docker inspect \
        --format "{{ .State.Pid }}" 93f5d72c2f21
2543
```

Apparently, from the preceding output, the process ID of the container `93f5d72c2f21` is `2543`.

3. Having got the process ID of the container, let's continue to see how the process associated with the container looks in the Docker host, using the `ps` command:

```
$ ps -fp 2543
UID          PID  PPID  C STIME TTY          TIME CMD
root        2543  6810  0 13:46 pts/7     00:00:00 /bin/bash
```

Amazing, isn't it? We launched a container with `/bin/bash` as its command, and we have the `/bin/bash` process in the Docker host as well.

4. Let's go one step further and display the `/proc/2543/environ` file in the Docker host using the `cat` command:

```
$ sudo cat -v /proc/2543/environ
PATH=/usr/local/sbin:/usr/local/bin:/usr/sbin:/usr/bin:/sbin:/
bin^@HOSTNAME=93f5d72c2f21^@TERM=xterm^@HOME=/root^@$
```

In the preceding output, `HOSTNAME=93f5d72c2f21` stands out from the other environment variables because `93f5d72c2f21` is the container ID, as well as the hostname of the container, which we launched previously.

5. Now, let's get back to the terminal, where we are running our interactive container `93f5d72c2f21`, and list all the processes running inside this container using the `ps` command:

```
root@93f5d72c2f21:/# ps -ef
UID       PID PPID C STIME TTY        TIME CMD
root        1   0 0 18:46 ?      00:00:00 /bin/bash
root       15   1 0 19:30 ?      00:00:00 ps -ef
```

Surprising, isn't it? Inside the container, the process ID of the `bin/bash` process is `1`, whereas outside the container, in the Docker host, the process ID is `2543`. Besides, the **Parent Process ID (PPID)** is `0` (zero).

In the Linux world, every system has just one root process with the PID 1 and PPID 0, which is the root of the complete process tree of that system. The Docker framework cleverly leverages the Linux PID namespace to spin a completely new process tree; thus, the processes running inside a container have no access to the parent process of the Docker host. However, the Docker host has a complete view of the child PID namespace spun by the Docker engine.

The network namespace ensures that all containers have independent network interfaces on the host machine. Also, each container has its own loopback interface. Each container talks to the outside world using its own network interface. You will be surprised to know that the namespace not only has its own routing table, but also has its own iptables, chains, and rules. The author of this chapter is running three containers on his host machine. Here, it is natural to expect three network interfaces for each container. Let's run the `docker ps` command:

```
$ sudo docker ps
41668be6e513        docker-apache2:latest    "/bin/sh -c 'apachec
069e73d4f63c        nginx:latest             "nginx -g '
871da6a6cf43        ubuntu:14.04             "/bin/bash"
```

So here, three are three interfaces, one for each container. Let's get their details by running the following command:

```
$ ifconfig
veth2d99bd3 Link encap:Ethernet  HWaddr 42:b2:cc:a5:d8:f3
          inet6 addr: fe80::40b2:ccff:fea5:d8f3/64 Scope:Link
          UP BROADCAST RUNNING  MTU:9001  Metric:1
veth422c684 Link encap:Ethernet  HWaddr 02:84:ab:68:42:bf
          inet6 addr: fe80::84:abff:fe68:42bf/64 Scope:Link
          UP BROADCAST RUNNING  MTU:9001  Metric:1
vethc359aec Link encap:Ethernet  HWaddr 06:be:35:47:0a:c4
          inet6 addr: fe80::4be:35ff:fe47:ac4/64 Scope:Link
          UP BROADCAST RUNNING  MTU:9001  Metric:1
```

The mount namespace ensures that the mounted filesystem is accessible only to the processes within the same namespace. The container A cannot see the mount points of the container B. If you want to check your mount points, you need to first log in to your container using the `exec` command (described in the next section), and then go to `/proc/mounts`:

```
root@871da6a6cf43:/# cat /proc/mounts
rootfs / rootfs rw 0 0/dev/mapper/docker-202:1-149807
871da6a6cf4320f625d5c96cc24f657b7b231fe89774e09fc771b3684bf405fb /
ext4 rw,relatime,discard,stripe=16,data=ordered 0 0 proc /proc proc
rw,nosuid,nodev,noexec,relatime 0 0
```

Let's run a container with a mount point that runs as the **Storage Area Network (SAN)** or **Network Attached Storage (NAS)** device and access it by logging into the container. This is given to you as an exercise. I have implemented this in one of my projects at work.

There are other namespaces that these containers/processes can be isolated into, namely, user, IPC, and UTS. The user namespace allows you to have root privileges within the namespace without giving that particular access to processes outside the namespace. Isolating a process with the IPC namespace gives it its own interprocess communication resources, for example, System V IPC and POSIX messages. The UTS namespace isolates the *hostname* of the system.

Docker has implemented this namespace using the `clone` system call. On the host machine, you can inspect the namespace created by Docker for the container (with pid 3728):

```
$ sudo ls /proc/3728/ns/
ipc  mnt  net  pid  user  uts
```

In most industrial deployments of Docker, people are extensively using patched Linux kernels to provide specific needs. Also, a few companies have patched their kernels to attach arbitrary processes to the existing namespaces because they feel that this is the most convenient and reliable way to deploy, control, and orchestrate containers.

Control groups

Linux containers rely on control groups (cgroups), which not only track groups of processes, but also expose metrics of the CPU, memory, and block I/O usage. You can access these metrics and obtain network usage metrics as well. Control groups are another important components of Linux containers. Control groups are around for a while and are initially merged in the Linux kernel code 2.6.24. They ensure that each Docker container will get a fixed amount of memory, CPU, and disk I/O, so that any container will not able to bring the host machine down at any point of time under any circumstances. Control groups do not play a role in preventing one container from being accessed, but they are essential to fending off some **Denial of Service (DoS)** attacks.

On Ubuntu 14.04, `cgroup` is implemented in the `/sys/fs/cgroup` path. The memory information of Docker is available at the `/sys/fs/cgroup/memory/docker/` path.

Similarly, the CPU details are made available in the `/sys/fs/cgroup/cpu/docker/` path.

Let's find out the maximum limit of memory that can be consumed by the container (`41668be6e513e845150abd2dd95dd574591912a7fda947f6744a0bfdb5cd9a85`).

For this, you can go to the `cgroup` memory path and check for the `memory.max.usage` file:

```
/sys/fs/cgroup/memory/docker/41668be6e513e845150abd2dd95dd574591912a7
fda947f6744a0bfdb5cd9a85
$ cat memory.max_usage_in_bytes
13824000
```

So, by default, any container can use up to 13.18 MB memory only.

Similarly, CPU parameters can be found in the following path:

```
/sys/fs/cgroup/cpu/docker/41668be6e513e845150abd2dd95dd574591912a7fda
947f6744a0bfdb5cd9a85
```

Traditionally, Docker runs only one process inside the containers.
So typically, you have seen people running three containers each for PHP, nginx, and MySQL. However, this is a myth. You can run all your three processes inside a single container.

Docker isolates many aspects of the underlying host from an application running in a container without the root privileges. However, this separation is not as strong as that of virtual machines, which run independent OS instances on top of a hypervisor without sharing the kernel with the underlying OS. It's not a good idea to run applications with different security profiles as containers on the same host, but there are security benefits to encapsulate different applications into containerized applications that would otherwise run directly on the same host.

Debugging a containerized application

Computer programs (software) sometimes fail to behave as expected. This is due to faulty code or due to the environmental changes between the development, testing, and deployment systems. Docker container technology eliminates the environmental issues between development, testing, and deployment as much as possible by containerizing all the application dependencies. Nonetheless, there could be still anomalies due to faulty code or variations in the kernel behavior, which needs debugging. Debugging is one of the most complex processes in the software engineering world and it becomes much more complex in the container paradigm because of the isolation techniques. In this section, we are going to learn a few tips and tricks to debug a containerized application using the tools native to Docker, as well as the tools provided by external sources.

Initially, many people in the Docker community individually developed their own debugging tools, but later Docker started supporting native tools, such as `exec`, `top`, `logs`, `events`, and many more. In this section, we will dive deep into the following Docker tools:

- `exec`
- `ps`
- `top`
- `stats`
- `events`
- `logs`

The Docker exec command

The `docker exec` command provided the much-needed help to users, who are deploying their own web servers or other applications running in the background. Now, it is not necessary to log in to run the SSH daemon in the container.

First, run the `docker ps -a` command to get the container ID:

```
$ sudo docker ps -a

b34019e5b5ee          nsinit:latest            "make local"

a245253db38b          training/webapp:latest   "python app.py"
```

Then, run the `docker exec` command to log in to the container.

```
$ sudo docker exec -it a245253db38b bash

root@a245253db38b:/opt/webapp#
```

It is important to note that the `docker exec` command can only access the running containers, so if the container stops functioning, then you need to restart the stopped container in order to proceed. The `docker exec` command spawns a new process in the target container using the Docker API and CLI. So if you run the `pe -aef` command inside the target container, it looks like this:

```
# ps -aef
UID          PID  PPID  C STIME TTY          TIME CMD
root           1     0  0 Mar22 ?        00:00:53 python app.py
root          45     0  0 18:11 ?        00:00:00 bash
root          53    45  0 18:11 ?        00:00:00 ps -aef
```

Here, `python app.y` is the application that is already running in the target container, and the `docker exec` command has added the `bash` process inside the container. If you run `kill -9 pid(45)`, you will be automatically logged out of the container.

If you are an enthusiastic developer, and you want to enhance the `exec` functionality, you can refer to `https://github.com/chris-rock/docker-exec`.

It is recommended that you use the `docker exec` command only for monitoring and diagnostic purposes, and I personally believe in the concept of one process per container, which is one of the best practices widely accentuated.

The Docker ps command

The docker ps command, which is available inside the container, is used to see the status of the process. This is similar to the standard ps command in the Linux environment and is *not* a docker ps command that we run on the Docker host machine.

This command runs inside the Docker container:

```
root@5562f2f29417:/# ps -s
  UID   PID   PENDING   BLOCKED   IGNORED    CAUGHT STAT TTY
TIME COMMAND
    0     1  00000000  00010000  00380004  4b817efb Ss   ?
0:00 /bin/bash
    0    33  00000000  00000000  00000000  73d3fef9 R+   ?
0:00 ps -s
root@5562f2f29417:/# ps -l
F S   UID   PID  PPID  C PRI  NI ADDR SZ WCHAN  TTY          TIME CMD
4 S     0     1     0  0  80   0 -  4541 wait   ?        00:00:00
bash
0 R     0    34     1  0  80   0 -  1783 -      ?        00:00:00 ps
root@5562f2f29417:/# ps -t
  PID TTY       STAT    TIME COMMAND
    1 ?         Ss      0:00 /bin/bash
   35 ?         R+      0:00 ps -t
root@5562f2f29417:/# ps -m
  PID TTY          TIME CMD
    1 ?        00:00:00 bash
    - -        00:00:00 -
   36 ?        00:00:00 ps
    - -        00:00:00 -
root@5562f2f29417:/# ps -a
  PID TTY          TIME CMD
   37 ?        00:00:00 ps
```

Use ps --help <simple|list|output|threads|misc|all> or ps --help <s|l|o|t|m|a> for additional help text.

The Docker top command

You can run the `top` command from the Docker host machine using the following command:

```
docker top [OPTIONS] CONTAINER [ps OPTIONS]
```

This gives a list of the running processes of a container without logging into the container, as follows:

```
$ sudo docker top   a245253db38b
UID                    PID             PPID            C
STIME                  TTY             TIME            CMD
root                   5232            3585            0
Mar22                  ?               00:00:53        python
app.py
$ sudo docker top   a245253db38b   -aef
UID                    PID             PPID            C
STIME                  TTY             TIME            CMD
root                   5232            3585            0
Mar22                  ?               00:00:53        python
app.py
```

The Docker `top` command provides information about the CPU, memory, and swap usage if you run it inside a Docker container:

```
root@a245253db38b:/opt/webapp# top
top - 19:35:03 up 25 days, 15:50,  0 users,  load average: 0.00,
0.01, 0.05
Tasks:   3 total,   1 running,   2 sleeping,   0 stopped,   0 zombie
Cpu(s):  0.0%us,  0.0%sy,  0.0%ni, 99.9%id,  0.0%wa,  0.0%hi,
0.0%si,  0.0%st
Mem:   1016292k total,    789812k used,    226480k free,     83280k
buffers
Swap:        0k total,        0k used,        0k free,    521972k
cached
  PID USER      PR  NI  VIRT  RES  SHR S %CPU %MEM    TIME+  COMMAND
    1 root      20   0 44780  10m 1280 S  0.0  1.1   0:53.69 python
   62 root      20   0 18040 1944 1492 S  0.0  0.2   0:00.01 bash
   77 root      20   0 17208 1164  948 R  0.0  0.1   0:00.00 top
```

In case you get the error `error - TERM environment variable not set` while running the `top` command inside the container, perform the following steps to resolve it:

Run the `echo $TERM` command. You will get the result as `dumb`. Then, run the following command:

```
$ export TERM=dumb
```

This will resolve the error.

The Docker stats command

The Docker `stats` command provides you with the capability to view the memory, CPU, and the network usage of a container from a Docker host machine, as illustrated here:

```
$ sudo docker stats a245253db38b
CONTAINER           CPU %                   MEM USAGE/LIMIT       MEM %
  NET I/O
a245253db38b        0.02%                   16.37 MiB/992.5 MiB   1.65%
  3.818 KiB/2.43 KiB
```

You can run the `stats` command to also view the usage for multiple containers:

```
$ sudo docker stats a245253db38b f71b26cee2f1
```

In the latest release of Docker 1.5, Docker provides you access to container statistics *read only* parameters. This will streamline the CPU, memory, network IO, and block IO of your containers. This helps you choose the resource limits and also in profiling. The Docker stats utility provides you with these resource usage details only for running containers. You can get detailed information using the end point APIs at `https://docs.docker.com/reference/api/docker_remote_api_v1.17/#inspect-a-container`.

Docker stats is originally taken from Michael Crosby's code contribution, which can be accessed at `https://github.com/crosbymichael`.

The Docker events command

Docker containers will report the following real-time events: create, destroy, die, export, kill, omm, pause, restart, start, stop, and unpause. The following are a few examples that illustrate how to use these commands:

```
$ sudo docker pause  a245253db38b

a245253db38b

$ sudo docker ps -a

a245253db38b          training/webapp:latest      "python app.py"
4 days ago           Up 4 days (Paused)         0.0.0.0:5000->5000/tcp
sad_sammet
$ sudo docker unpause  a245253db38b

a245253db38b

$ sudo docker ps -a

a245253db38b          training/webapp:latest      "python app.py"
4 days ago     Up 4 days           0.0.0.0:5000->5000/tcp    sad_sammet
```

The Docker image will also report the untag and delete events.

Using multiple filters will be handled as an AND operation; for example, --filter container= a245253db38b --filter event=start will display events for the container a245253db38b and the event type is start.

Currently, the supported filters are container, event, and image.

The Docker logs command

This command fetches the log of a container without logging into the container. It batch-retrieves logs present at the time of execution. These logs are the output of STDOUT and STDERR. The general usage is shown in docker logs [OPTIONS] CONTAINER.

The -follow option will continue to provide the output till the end, -t will provide the timestamp, and --tail= <number of lines> will show the number of lines of the log messages of your container:

```
$ sudo docker logs a245253db38b
 * Running on http://0.0.0.0:5000/
172.17.42.1 - - [22/Mar/2015 06:04:23] "GET / HTTP/1.1" 200 -
```

```
172.17.42.1 - - [24/Mar/2015 13:43:32] "GET / HTTP/1.1" 200 -
$

$ sudo docker logs -t a245253db38b

2015-03-22T05:03:16.866547111Z  * Running on http://0.0.0.0:5000/

2015-03-22T06:04:23.349691099Z 172.17.42.1 - - [22/Mar/2015 06:04:23]
"GET / HTTP/1.1" 200 -

2015-03-24T13:43:32.754295010Z 172.17.42.1 - - [24/Mar/2015 13:43:32]
"GET / HTTP/1.1" 200 -
```

We also used the docker logs utility in *Chapter 2*, *Handling Docker Containers* and *Chapter 6*, *Running Services in a Container*, to view the logs of our containers.

Installing and using nsenter

In any commercial Docker deployments, you may use various containers, such as web application, database, and so on. However, you need to access these containers in order to modify the configuration or debug/troubleshoot the issues. A simple solution for this problem is to run an SSH server in each container. It is a not good way to access the machines due to unanticipated security implications. However, if you are working in any one of the world-class IT companies, such as IBM, DELL, HP, and so on, your security compliance guy will never allow you to use SSH to connect to machines.

So, here is the solution. The nsenter tool provides you access to log in to your container. Note that nsenter will be first deployed as a Docker container only. Using this deployed nsenter, you can access your container. Follow these steps:

1. Let's run a simple web application as a container:

    ```
    $ sudo docker run -d -p 5000:5000 training/webapp python
    app.py
    -----------------------
    a245253db38b626b8ac4a05575aa704374d0a3c25a392e0f4f562df92bb98d
    74
    ```

2. Test the web container:

    ```
    $ curl localhost:5000
    Hello world!
    ```

3. Install nsenter and run it as a container:

    ```
    $ sudo docker run -v /usr/local/bin:/target jpetazzo/nsenter
    ```

    Now, nsenter is up and running as a container.

4. Use the nsenter container to log in to the container (a245253db38b), that we created in step 1.

Run the following command to get the PID value:

```
$ PID=$(sudo docker inspect --format {{.State.Pid}}
a245253db38b)
```

5. Now, access the web container:

```
$ sudo nsenter --target $PID --mount --uts --ipc --net --pid
root@a245253db38b:/#
```

Then, you can log in and start accessing your container. Accessing your container in this way will make your security and compliance professionals happy, and they will feel relaxed.

Since Docker 1.3, the Docker exec is a supported tool used for logging into containers.

The nsenter tool doesn't enter cgroups and therefore evades resource limitations. The potential benefit of this would be debugging and external audit, but for a remote access, docker exec is the current recommended approach.

The nsenter tool is tested only on Intel 64-bit platforms. You cannot run nsenter inside the container that you want to access, and hence, you need to run nsenter on host machines only. By running nsenter on a host machine, you can access all of the containers of that host machine. Also, you cannot use the running nsenter on a particular host, say host A to access the containers on host B.

Summary

Docker provides you with the isolation of containers using the Linux container technology, such as LXC and now libcontainer. Libcontainer is Docker's own implementation in the Go programming language to access the kernel namespace and control groups. This namespace is used for process-level isolation, while control groups is used for restricting the resource usage of running containers. Since the containers run as independent processes directly over the Linux kernel, the **generally available (GA)** debugging tools are not fit enough to work inside the containers to debug the containerized processes. Docker now provides you with a rich set of tools to effectively debug the container, as well as processes inside the container itself. Docker exec will allow you to log in to the container without running an SSH daemon in the container.

Docker `stats` provides information about the container's memory and CPU usage. Docker `events` reports the events, such as create, destroy, kill, and so on. Similarly, Docker `logs` fetch the logs from the container without logging into the container.

Debugging is the foundation that can be used to strategize other security vulnerabilities and holes. The next chapter is therefore incorporated to expound the plausible security threats of Docker containers and how they can be subdued with a variety of security approaches, automated tools, best practices, key guidelines, and metrics.

11
Securing Docker Containers

So far, we have talked a lot about the fast emerging Docker technology in this book. It is not a nice and neat finish if Docker-specific security issues and solution approaches are not articulated in detail to you. Hence, this chapter is specially crafted and incorporated in this book in order to explain about the growing security challenges of Docker-inspired containers. We also wanted to throw more light on how lingering security concerns are being addressed through a host of pioneering technologies, high-quality algorithms, enabling tools, and best practices.

In this chapter, we are going to deal with the following topics in detail:

- Are Docker containers secure?
- The security features of containers
- The emerging security approaches
- The best practices for container security

Ensuring unbreakable and impenctrable security for any IT system and business services has been one of the prime needs and predominant challenges in the IT field for decades. Brilliant minds can identify and exploit all kinds of security holes and flaws being carelessly and unknowingly introduced at the system conceptualization and concretization stages. This loophole ultimately brings innumerable breaches and havocs during IT service delivery. Security experts and engineers, on the other hand, try out every kind of trick and technique in order to stop hackers in their evil journey. However, it has not been an outright victory so far. Here and there, there are some noteworthy intrusions from unknown sources, resulting in highly disconcerting IT slowdown and sometimes breakdown. Organizations and governments across the globe are, therefore, investing heavily in security research endeavors in order to completely decimate all security and safety-related incidents and accidents.

There are plenty-of security-specific product vendors and managed security service providers in order to minimize the irreparable and indescribable consequences of security threats and vulnerabilities on IT systems. Precisely speaking, for any existing and emerging technologies, security is the most crucial and critical aspect, which is not to be taken lightly.

Docker is a fast-maturing containerization technology in the IT space, and in the recent past, the aspect of security is being given prime importance, considering the fact that the adoption and adaption of Docker containers is consistently on the rise. Furthermore, a stream of purpose-specific and generic containers are moving into production environments and hence, the security conundrum acquires a special significance. Undoubtedly, there will be a lot focus on the security parameters in future Docker platform releases, as the market and mind shares for this open source Docker initiative are consistently on the climb.

Are Docker containers secure enough?

With Docker containers being meticulously evaluated for production IT environments, there are questions being asked in different quarters about the security vulnerabilities of containers. Therefore, there is a clarion call to researchers and security experts for substantially strengthening container security in order to boost the confidence of service providers and consumers. In this section, we are going to describe where Docker containers stand as far as the security imbroglio is concerned. As containers are being closely examined in synchronization with virtual machines, we will start with a few security-related points of **virtual machines** (**VMs**) and containers.

The security facets – virtual machines versus Docker containers

Let's start with understanding how virtual machines differ from containers. Typically, virtual machines are heavyweight, and hence bloated, whereas containers are lightweight, and hence, slim and sleek.

The following table captures the renowned qualities of VMs and containers:

Virtual Machines	Containers
A few VMs can run together on a single physical machine (low density).	Tens of containers can run on a single physical or virtual machine (high density).
This ensures the complete isolation of VMs for security.	This enables isolation at the process level and provides additional isolation using features, such as namespaces and cgroups.
Each VM has its own OS and the physical resources are managed by an underlying hypervisor.	Containers share the same kernel as their Docker host.
For networking, VMs can be linked to virtual or physical switches. Hypervisors have buffer for I/O performance improvement, NIC bonding, and so on.	Containers leverage standard IPC mechanisms, such as signals, pipes, sockets, and so on, for networking. Each container gets its own network stack.

The following diagram clearly illustrates the structural differences between the matured virtualization paradigm and the fast-evolving containerization idea:

The debate on the security-side of VMs and containers is heating up. There are arguments and counter arguments in favor of one or the other. The preceding diagram helps us visualize, compare, and contrast the security implications in both paradigms.

In the case of the virtualization paradigm, the hypervisors are the centralized and core controllers of the virtual machines. Any kind of access to freshly provisioned virtual machines needs to go through this hypervisor solution, which stands as a solid wall for any kind of unauthenticated, unauthorized, and unethical purposes. Therefore, the attack surface of a virtual machine is smaller in comparison to containers. The hypervisor has to be hacked or broken into in order to impact other VMs.

In contrast to the virtualization paradigm, the containers are placed directly on top of the kernel of the host system. This lean and mean architecture gives a much higher efficiency because it completely eliminates the emulation layer of a hypervisor and also offers a much higher container density. However, unlike the virtual machine paradigm, the container paradigm does not have many layers, so one can easily gain access to the host and other containers if any of the containers is compromised. Therefore, the attack surface of a container is larger in comparison to virtual machines.

However, the designers of the Docker platform have given due consideration to this security risk and designed the system to thwart most security risks. In the ensuing sections, we will discuss the security that is innately designed in the system, the solutions being prescribed to substantially enhance the container security, and the best practices and guidelines.

The security features of containers

Linux containers, especially Docker containers, have a few interesting innate security-fulfilling features. Therefore, the containerization movement is blessed with decent security. In this section, we will discuss these security-related features in detail.

The Docker platform promotes a layered security approach to bring in more decisive and deft security for containers, as shown in the following diagram:

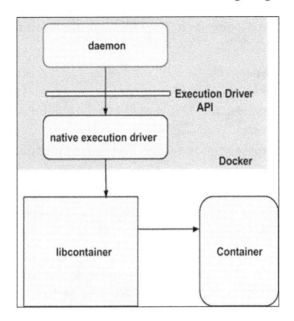

As discussed, Docker uses a host of security barricades to stop breaches. That is, if one security mechanism gets broken, other mechanisms quickly come in the way of containers being hacked. There are a few key areas that are to be examined when evaluating the security implications of Docker containers.

Resource isolation

As we all know, containers are being positioned for the era of the microservices architecture. That is, in a single system, there can be multiple generic, as well as purpose-specific, services that dynamically collaborate with one another for realizing easy-to-sustain distributed applications. With the multiplicity and heterogeneity of services in a physical system on the climb, it is unsurprising that security complexity is bound to shoot up. Therefore, resources need to be clearly demarcated and isolated in order to escape from any kind of perilous security breach. The widely accepted security approach is to leverage the kernel feature of namespaces.

The kernel namespaces guarantee the much-needed isolation feature for Linux containers. The Docker project has added a few additional namespaces for Docker containers, and each distinct aspect of a container runs in its own namespace and hence, does not have access outside it. The following is a list of namespaces that Docker uses:

- **The PID namespace**: This is used for a series of actions taken in order to achieve process-level isolation

- **The Network namespace**: This is used to have executive control over the network interfaces

- **The IPC namespace**: This is used to maintain control over access to IPC resources

- **The Mount namespace**: This is used to manage mount points

- **The UTS namespace**: This is used to segregate the kernel and version identifiers

Kernel namespaces provide the first and foremost form of isolation. Processes running in a container don't affect processes running in another container or in the host system. The network namespace ensures that each container gets its own network stack, thus restricting access to the interfaces of other containers. From the network architecture point of view, all the containers on a given Docker host are sitting on bridge interfaces. This means that they are just like physical machines connected to a common Ethernet switch.

Resource accounting and control

Containers consume different physical resources in order to deliver their unique capabilities. However, the resource consumption has to be disciplined, orderly, and hence, critically regulated. When there is a deviation, there is a greater possibility of invalidating the containers from performing their assigned tasks in time. For example, **Denial of Service (DoS)** results if the resource usage is not systematically synchronized.

The Linux containers leverage control groups (cgroups) to implement resource accounting and auditing to run applications in a frictionless manner. As we all know, there are multiple resources that contribute to running the containers successfully. They provide many useful metrics and ensure that each container gets its fair share of memory, CPU, and disk I/O.

Furthermore, they guarantee that a single container cannot bring the system down by exhausting any one of these resources. This feature helps you fend off some DoS attacks. This feature helps in running containers as multi-tenant citizens in cloud environments to ensure their uptime and performance. Any kind of exploitation by other containers are identified proactively and nipped in the bud so that any kind of misadventure gets avoided.

The root privilege – impacts and best practices

The Docker engine efficiently protects the containers from any malicious activities by leveraging the recently mentioned resource isolation and control techniques. Nonetheless, Docker exposes a few potential security threats because the Docker daemon runs with the root privilege. Here, in this section, we list a few security risks and the best practices to mitigate them.

The trusted user control

Since the Docker daemon runs with the root privilege, it has the capability to mount any directory from the Docker host to the container, without limiting any access rights. That is, you can start a container, where the /host directory will be the / directory on your host, and the container will be able to alter your host filesystem without any restriction. This is just an example among a myriad of malicious uses. Considering these activities, latter versions of Docker restrict access to the Docker daemon through a Unix socket. Docker can be configured to access the daemon through the REST API over HTTP, if you explicitly decide to do so. However, you should ensure that it will be reachable only from a trusted network or VPN or protected with stunnel and client SSL certificates. You can also secure them with HTTPS and certificates.

Non-root containers

As mentioned previously, the Docker containers, by default, run with the root privilege and so does the application that runs inside the container. This is another major concern from a security perspective because hackers can gain root access to the Docker host by hacking the application running inside the container. Do not despair, Docker provides a simple yet powerful solution to change the container's privilege to a non-root user, thus, thwarting malicious root access to the Docker host. This change to non-root user can be accomplished using the -u or --user option of the docker run subcommand or the USER instruction in the Dockerfile.

In this section, we will demonstrate this concept by showing you the default root privilege of the Docker container and then, continue to modify the root privilege to a non-root user using the USER instruction in the Dockerfile.

First, we demonstrate the default root privilege of the Docker container by running a simple id command in a docker run subcommand, as shown here:

```
$ sudo docker run --rm ubuntu:14.04 id
uid=0(root) gid=0(root) groups=0(root)
```

Now, let's perform the following steps:

1. Craft a Dockerfile that creates a non-root privilege user and modify the default root user to the newly-created non-root privilege user, as shown here:

    ```
    #######################################################
    # Dockerfile to change from root to non root privilege
    #######################################################

    # Base image is Ubuntu
    FROM ubuntu:14.04

    # Add a new user "peter" with user id 7373
    RUN useradd -u 7373  peter

    # Change to non-root privilege
    USER peter
    uid=0(root) gid=0(root) groups=0(root)
    ```

2. Proceed to build the Docker image using the docker build subcommand, as depicted here:

    ```
    $ sudo docker build -t nonrootimage .
    ```

3. Finally, let's verify the current user of the container, using the id command in a docker run subcommand:

    ```
    $ sudo docker run --rm nonrootimage id
    uid=7373(peter) gid=7373(peter) groups=7373(peter)
    ```

Evidently, the container's user, group, the groups are now changed to a non-root user.

Modifying the default root privilege to a non-root privilege is a very effective way of containing malevolent penetration into the Docker host kernel.

Loading the Docker images and the security implications

Docker typically pulls images from the network, which are usually curated and verified at the source. However, for the purpose of backup and restore, the Docker images can be saved using the `docker save` subcommand and loaded back using the `docker load` subcommand. This mechanism can also be used to load third-party images through unconventional means. Unfortunately, in such a practice, the Docker engine cannot verify the source and hence, the images can carry malicious code. So, as a first shield of safety, Docker extracts the image in a chrooted subprocess for privilege separation. Even though Docker ensures the privilege separation, it is not recommended to load arbitrary images.

The emerging security approaches

So far, we have discussed the unique security-related kernel characteristics and capabilities. Most security holes can be closed down by understanding and applying those kernel capabilities. Security experts and exponents, having considered the faster and widespread adoption of the raging containerization idea in production environments, have brought forth a few more additional security solutions, which we will describe in detail. These security methods need to be given utmost importance by developers as well as system administrators while developing, deploying, and delivering enterprise-class containers in order to nullify any kind of inside or outside security attack.

Security-Enhanced Linux for container security

Security-Enhanced Linux (**SELinux**) is a brave attempt to clean up the security holes in Linux containers and is an implementation of a **Mandatory Access Control** (**MAC**) mechanism, **Multi-Level security** (**MLS**), and **Multi-Category security** (**MCS**) in the Linux kernel. A new collaborative initiative referred to as Virtproject, is being built on SELinux, and this is getting integrated with Libvirt to provide an adaptable MAC framework for virtual machines, as well as containers. This new architecture provides a sheltered separation and safety net for containers, as it primarily prevents root processes within the container from interfacing and interfering with other processes running outside this container. Docker containers are automatically assigned to an SELinux context specified in the SELinux policy.

SELinux always checks for all the allowed operations after the standard **discretionary access control (DAC)** is completely checked. SELinux can establish and enforce rules on files and processes in a Linux system and on their actions based on defined policies. As per SELinux specification, files, including directories and devices, are referred to as objects. Similarly, processes, such as a user running a command, are being termed as subjects. Most operating systems use a DAC system that controls how subjects interact with objects and one another. Using DAC on operating systems, users can control the permissions of their own objects. For example, on a Linux OS, users can make their home directories readable, giving users and subjects a handle to steal potentially sensitive information. However, DAC alone is not a fool-proof security method and DAC access decisions are solely based on user identity and ownership. Generally, DAC simply ignores other security enabling parameters, such as the role of the user, the function, the trustworthiness of the program, and the sensitivity and integrity of the data.

As each user typically has complete discretion over their files, ensuring a system-wide security policy is difficult. Furthermore, every program run by a user simply inherits all the permissions granted to the user, and the user is free to change the access to his/her files. All these lead to a minimal protection against malicious software. Many system services and privileged programs run with coarse-grained privileges so that any flaw in any one of these programs can be easily exploited and extended to gain catastrophic access to the system.

As mentioned at the beginning, SELinux adds **Mandatory Access Control (MAC)** to the Linux kernel. This means that the owners of an object have no control or discretion over access to an object. The kernel enforces MAC which is a general-purpose MAC mechanism and it needs the ability to enforce administratively-set security policies to all the processes and files in the system. These files and processes will be used to base decisions on labels containing a variety of security-centric information. MAC has the inherent capability to sufficiently protect the system. Furthermore, MAC ensures application security against any willful hacking and tampering. MAC also provides a strong separation of applications so that any attacked and compromised application runs separately.

Next in line is the **Multi-Category Security (MCS)**. MCS is mainly used to protect containers from other containers. That is, any affected container does not have the capability to bring down other containers in the same Docker host. MCS is based on the Multi-Level Security (MLS) capability and uniquely takes advantage of the last component of the SELinux label, *the MLS Field*. In general, when containers are launched, the Docker daemon picks a random MCS label. The Docker daemon labels all of the content in the container with that MCS label.

When the daemon launches the container process, it tells the kernel to label the processes with the same MCS label. The kernel only allows container processes to read/write their own content as long as the process MCS label matches the filesystem content MCS label. The kernel blocks the container processes from reading/writing content that is labeled with a different MCS label. This way, a hacked container process is prevented from attacking different containers. The Docker daemon is responsible for guaranteeing that no containers use the same MCS label. The cascading of errors among containers is prohibited through the adroit usage of MCS.

SELinux-inspired benefits

SELinux is being positioned as one of the major improvements to bring foolproof security to Docker containers. It is abundantly clear that there are several security-related advantages with SELinux. As Docker containers natively run on Linux systems, the core and critical advancements being made in Linux systems through the elegant SELinux approach are easily replicated for Docker containers too. All processes and files are accordingly labeled with a type. A type is capable of defining and differentiating a domain for processes and a distinct domain for files. Processes are fully separated from each other by running them in their own domains, and any incursion into others is stringently monitored and nipped in the budding stage itself. SELinux empowers us to establish and enforce policy rules to define how processes interact with files and with each other. For example, any access is allowed only if there is a clearly articulated SELinux policy to allow the desired and demarcated access. Precisely speaking, SELinux can come handy in enforcing data confidentiality and integrity. SELinux is also beneficial for protecting processes from untrusted inputs. It comes with the following benefits:

- **Fine-grained access control**: SELinux access decisions are based on considering all kinds of security-impacting information, such as a SELinux user, role, type, and level. SELinux policy can be administratively defined, enforced, and enacted at a system level. User discretion in loosening and lightening security and access policies is totally eliminated with the comprehensive leverage of the SELinux upgrade.

- **Reduced vulnerability to privilege escalation attacks**: These processes generally run in domains and are therefore cleanly separated from each other. SELinux policy rules define how processes can access files and other processes. That is, if a process is advertently or unknowingly compromised, the attacker only has access to the standard functions of that process and to the files the process has been configured to have access to. For example, if a web server is brought down, an attacker cannot use that process to read other files, unless a specific SELinux policy rule was incorporated to allow such access.

- **Process separation in SELinux**: These processes are slated to run in their own domains, preventing processes from accessing files used by other processes, as well as preventing processes from accessing other processes. For example, when running SELinux, an attacker cannot compromise a server module (for instance, Samba Server) and then use that as an attack vector to read and write to files used by other processes, such as backend databases. SELinux comes in handy in substantially limiting the damage made by improper configuration mistakes. Domain Name System (DNS) servers often replicate information between each other and this is called as a zone transfer. Attackers can use zone transfers to update DNS servers with false information. SELinux prevents zone files being misused by any hackers. We use two types of SELinux enforcement for Docker containers.

- **Type enforcement**: This protects the host from the processes within the container. The default type for running Docker containers is `svirt_lxc_net_t`. All container processes run with this type, and all the content within the container is labeled with the `svirt_sandbox_file_t` type. The `svirt_lxc_net_t` default type is allowed to manage any content labeled with `svirt_sandbox_file_t`. Furthermore, `svirt_lxc_net_t` is also able to read/execute most labels under `/usr` on the host.

- **A security problem**: If all container processes are run with `svirt_lxc_net_t` and all the content is labeled with `svirt_sandbox_file_t`, container processes may be allowed to attack processes running in other containers and content owned by other containers. This is where Multi Category Security (MCS) enforcement comes in handy.

- **Multi-Category Security (MCS)**: This is a solid enhancement to SELinux that allows users to label files with categories. These categories are actually used to further constrain **Discretionary Access Control (DAC)** and **Type Enforcement (TE)** logic. An example of a category is *Company_Confidential*. Only users with access to this category can access files labeled with the category, assuming that the existing DAC and TE rules also permit access. The term *categories* refers to the same nonhierarchical categories used by **Multi-Level Security (MLS)**. Under MLS, objects and subjects are labeled with security levels. These security levels consist of a hierarchical sensitivity value, such as *Top Secret*, and zero or more nonhierarchical categories, such as *Crypto*. Categories provide compartments within the sensitivity levels and enforce the need-to-know security principle. MCS is an adaptation of MLS and represents a policy change. Beyond the access control, MCS can be used to display the MCS categories at the top and bottom of the printed pages. This may also include a cover sheet to indicate the document handling procedures.

- **AppArmor**: This is an effective and easy-to-use Linux application security system. AppArmor proactively protects the OS and applications from any external or internal threats, even zero-day attacks, by enforcing good behavior and preventing even unknown application flaws from being exploited. AppArmor security policies completely define what system resources individual applications can access and with what privileges. A number of default policies are included in AppArmor, and using a combination of advanced static analysis and learning-based tools, AppArmor policies, for even very complex applications, can be deployed successfully in a matter of hours. AppArmor is available for Docker containers, on systems that support it. AppArmor provides enterprise-class, host-intrusion prevention, and protects the operating system and applications from the harmful effects of internal or external attacks, malicious applications, and viruses. As a result, businesses can protect mission-critical data, reduce system administration costs, and ensure compliance with government regulations. Comprehensive enterprise-wide network application security requires attention to both users and applications. This is one prominent option available to bring in impenetrable security for Docker containers and applications present inside the containers. Policies are turning out to be a powerful mechanism in ensuring container security. Policy formulation and the automated enforcement of policies go a long way in guaranteeing the safety of containers.

The best practices for container security

There are robust and resilient security solutions to boost the confidence of providers, as well as users, toward embracing the containerization journey with all the clarity and alacrity. In this section, we provide a number of tips, best practices, and key guidelines collected from different sources in order to enable security administrators and consultants to tightly secure Docker containers. Essentially, if containers are running in a multitenant system and you are not using the proven security practices, then there are definite dangers lurking around the security front. As mentioned previously, security breaches can happen at different service levels and hence, security architects need to figure out what can go wrong and prescribe proven and pioneering security-preserving methods. Security visionaries and luminaries advise the following easy-to-understand-and-follow practices to reap the originally envisaged benefits of containers:

- Do away with the privileged access
- Run your containers and services as non-root as much as possible

The first and foremost advice is not to run random and untested Docker images on your system. Strategize and leverage trusted repositories of Docker images and containers to subscribe and use applications and data containers for application development, packaging, shipping, deployment, and delivery. It is clear from past experiences that any untrusted containers that are downloaded from the public domain may result in malevolent and messy situations. Linux distributions, such as **Red Hat Enterprise Linux (RHEL)**, have the following mechanisms in place in order to assist administrators to ensure the utmost security:

- A trusted repository of software to be downloaded and used
- Security updates and patches to fix vulnerabilities
- A security response team to find and manage vulnerabilities
- A team of engineers to manage/maintain packages and work on security enhancements
- Common criteria certification to check the security of the operating system

As mentioned previously, the biggest problem is that not everything in Linux is namespaced. Currently, Docker uses five namespaces to alter the process' view of any system—process, network, mount, hostname, and shared memory. While these give the users some level of security, it is by no means a comprehensive one such as KVM. In a KVM environment, processes in a virtual machine do not talk to the host kernel directly. They do not have any access to kernel filesystems. Device nodes can talk to the VMs kernel, but not to hosts. Therefore, in order to have a privilege escalation out of a VM, the process has to subvert the VM's kernel, find an enabling vulnerability in the hypervisor, break through SELinux Controls (sVirt), and attack the host's kernel. In the container landscape, the approach is to protect the host from the processes within the container and to protect containers from other containers. It is all about the combination or clustering together of multiple security controls to defend containers and their contents.

Basically, we want to put in as many security barriers as possible to prevent any sort of break out. If a privileged process can break out of one containment mechanism, the idea is to block them with the next barrier in the hierarchy. With Docker, it is possible to take advantage of as many security mechanisms of Linux as possible.

The following are possible security measures that can be taken:

- **Filesystem protections**: Filesystems need to be read-only in order to escape from any kind of unauthorized write. That is, privileged container processes cannot write to them and do not affect the host system either. Generally, most of the applications need not write anything to their filesystems. There are several Linux distributions with read-only filesystems. It is therefore possible to block the ability of the privileged container processes from remounting filesystems as read and write. It is all about blocking the ability to mount any filesystems within the container.

- **Copy-on-write filesystems**: Docker has been using **Advanced Multi-layered unification Filesystem (AuFS)** as a filesystem for containers. AuFS is a layered filesystem that can transparently overlay one or more existing filesystems. When a process needs to modify a file, AuFS first creates a copy of that file and is capable of merging multiple layers into a single representation of a filesystem. This process is called copy-on-write, and this prevents one container from seeing the changes of another container even if they write to the same filesystem image. One container cannot change the image content to affect the processes in another container.

- **The choice of capabilities**: Typically, there are two ways to perform permission checks: privileged processes and unprivileged processes. Privileged processes bypass all sorts of kernel permission checks, while unprivileged processes are subject to full permission checking based on the process's credentials. The recent Linux kernel divides the privileges traditionally associated with the super-user into distinct units known as capabilities, which can be independently enabled and disabled. Capabilities are a per-thread attribute. Removing capabilities can bring forth several positive changes in Docker containers. Invariably, capabilities decide the Docker functionality, accessibility, usability, security, and so on. Therefore, it requires much thought while embarking on the journey of addition, as well as removal of capabilities.

- **Keeping systems and data secure**: Some security issues need to be addressed before enterprises and service providers use containers in production environments. Containerization will eventually make it easier to secure applications for the following three reasons:
    - A smaller payload reduces the surface area for security flaws
    - Instead of incrementally patching the operating system, you can update it
    - By allowing a clear separation of concerns, containers help IT and application teams collaborate purposefully

The IT department is responsible for the security flaws associated with the infrastructure. The application team fixes flaws inside the container and is also responsible for runtime dependencies. Easing the tension between IT and applications development teams helps smooth the transition to a hybrid cloud model. The responsibilities of each team are clearly demarcated in order to secure both containers and their runtime infrastructures. With such a clear segregation, proactively identifying any visible and invisible endangering security ordeals and promptly eliminating it in time, policy engineering and enforcement, precise and perfect configuration, leveraging appropriate security-unearthing and mitigation tools, and so on, are being systematically accomplished.

- **Leverage linux kernel capabilities**: An average server (bare metal or virtual machine) needs to run a bunch of processes as root. These typically include `ssh`, `cron`, `syslogd`, hardware management tools (for example, load modules), network configuration tools (for example, handling DHCP, WPA, or VPNs), and so on. A container is very different because almost all of these tasks are being handled by the infrastructures on which containers are to be hosted and run. There are several best practices, key guidelines, technical knowhow, and so on, on various blogs authored by security experts. You can find some of the most interesting and inspiring security-related details at `https://docs.docker.com/articles/security/`.

Digital signature verification

Docker, the popular open source container company, has announced that it has added the digital signature verification to Docker images. This will ensure that when you download a containerized application from an official Docker repository, you get the real version. At this point in time, the Docker engine automatically checks the provenance and integrity of all the images in the official repository using digital signatures. A digital signature brings on an additional trust on Docker images. That is, the particular Docker image was not tampered or twisted, and hence, it is ready to be fully used with all the confidence and clarity.

This newly-added cryptographic verification is used to provide users with an additional assurance of security. In the future, there will be features, such as publisher authentication, image integrity and authorization, **public key infrastructure** (**PKI**) management, and many more for both image publishers, as well as consumers. If an official image is corrupted or tampered with, Docker will instantaneously issue a warning. At this point in time, the Docker engine will not prevent any affected images from running and nonofficial images are not verified either. This will change the future versions as the Docker community hardens the code and irons out the inevitable usability quirks.

When developing an application, you sometimes need to take a look at it while it is running. A number of tools, such as `nsinit` and `nsenter`, have sprung up recently to help developers debug their containerized applications. Some users have taken to running an init process to spawn `sshd` along with their application to allow them access, which creates risk and overhead.

Secure deployment guidelines for Docker

Docker containers are increasingly hosted in production environments to be publicly discovered and used by many. Especially, with the faster adoption of cloud technologies, the IT environments of worldwide organizations and institutions are getting methodically optimized and transformed to deftly and decisively host a wider variety of virtual machines and containers. There are new improvements and enablements, such as Flocker and Clocker, in order to speed up the process of taking containers to cloud environments (private, public, hybrid, and community). There are recommendations that have to be followed while deploying containers. As we all know, containers remarkably reduce the overhead by allowing developers and system administrators to seamlessly deploy containers for applications and services required for business operations. However, because Docker leverages the same kernel as the host system to reduce the need for resources, containers can be exposed to significant security risks if not adequately configured. There are a few carefully annotated guidelines to be strictly followed by both developers and system administrators while deploying containers. For example, `https://github.com/GDSSecurity/Docker-Secure-Deployment-Guidelines` elaborates in a tabular form with all the right details.

It is an indisputable truth that the software flaws in distributed and complex applications open the way for intelligent attackers and hackers to break into systems that host critical, confidential, and customer data. Therefore, security solutions are being insisted and ingrained across all the layers in the IT stack, and hence, there arises many types of security vulnerabilities at different levels and layers. For example, perimeter security solves only part of the problem because the changing requirements are mandate for allowing network access to employees, customers, and partners. Similarly, there are firewalls, intrusion detection and prevention systems, application delivery controllers (ADCs), access controls, multifactor authentication and authorization, patching, and so on. Then, for securing data while in transit, persistence, and being used by applications, there are encryption, steganography, and hybrid security models. All these are reactive and realistic mechanisms, but the increasing tendency is all about virtual businesses insisting on proactive and preemptive security methods. As IT is tending and trending toward the much-anticipated virtual IT world, the security issues and implications are being given extra importance by security experts.

The future

There will be many more noteworthy improvisations, transformations, and disruptions in the containerization space in the days to come. Through a host of innovations and integrations, the Docker platform is being positioned as the leading one for strengthening the containerization journey. The following are the prime accomplishments through the smart leverage of the Docker technology:

- **Strengthening the distributed paradigm**: While computing is going to be increasingly distributed and federated, the microservices architecture (MSA) will play a very decisive and deeper role in IT. Docker containers are emerging as the most efficient ones for hosting and delivering a growing array of microservices. With container orchestration technologies and tools gaining greater recognition, microservices (specific, as well as generic) get identified, matched, orchestrated, and choreographed to form business-aware composite services.

- **Empowering the cloud paradigm**: The cloud idea is strongly gripping the IT world to bring in the much-insisted IT infrastructure rationalization, simplification, standardization, automation, and optimization. The abstraction and virtualization concepts, which are the key to the unprecedented success of the cloud paradigm, are penetrating into every kind of IT module. Originally, it started with server virtualization and now, it is all about storage and networking virtualization. With all the technological advancements around us, there is a widespread keenness to realize software-defined infrastructures (software-defined compute, storage, and networking). The Docker engine, the core and critical portion of the Docker platform, is duly solidified in order to bring in the necessary eligibility for containers to run on software-defined environments without any hitch or hurdle.

- **Enabling the IT elasticity, portability, agility, and adaptability**: Containers are emerging as the flexible and futuristic IT building blocks for bringing in more resiliency, versatility, elegance, and suppleness. The faster provisioning of IT resources to ensure higher availability and real-time scalability, the easy elimination of all kinds of frictions between development and operation teams, the guarantee of native performance of IT, the realization of organized and optimized IT for enhanced IT productivity, and so on are some of the exemplary things being visualized for Docker containers toward the smarter IT.

 Containers will be a strategic addition to virtual machines (VMs) and bare metal servers in order to bring in deeper IT automation, acceleration, and augmentation, thereby the much-hyped and hoped business agility, autonomy, and affordability will be achieved.

Summary

Security is definitely a challenge and an important aspect not to be sidestepped. If a container gets compromised, then bringing down the container host is not a difficult task. Thus, ensuring security for containers and then hosts is indispensable to the flourishing of the containerization concept, especially when the centralization and federation of IT systems is on the rise. In this chapter, we specifically focused on the sickening and devastating security issues of Docker containers and explained the ways and means of having foolproof security solutions for containers that host dynamic, enterprise-class, and mission-critical applications. In the days to come, there will be fresh security approaches and solutions in order to ensure impenetrable and unbreakable security for Docker containers and hosts, as the security of containers and their contents is of utmost importance to service providers, as well as consumers.

Index

N

Network Address Translation (NAT) 99
Network Attached Storage (NAS) 179
network configuration lists, container
       networking
  bridge 92
  gateway 92
  IP address 92
  IPPrefixLen 92
  PortMapping 92
  ports 92
Network namespace 196
Node.js 145
nsenter
  about 187
  installing 187
  using 188

O

ONBUILD instruction 55
orchestration, of containers
  about 138-140
  common usage 145-150
  docker-compose command 144
  docker-compose tool, installing 141, 142
  docker-compose tool, used 140
  docker-compose.yml file 142

P

Parent Process ID (PPID) 177
PID namespace 196
portability
  enabling 208
PortBindings object 101
Ports object 101
private repositories, Docker Hub 71
process level isolation, for Docker
       containers
  about 176
  control groups (cgroups) 180
  providing 176-179
public key infrastructure (PKI) 206
Python Web Server Gateway Interface
       (WSGI) HTTP server 81

R

Redis 145
repository management, Docker Hub
  library repository, creating 74
  library repository, deleting 74
  library repository images, listing 75
  library repository images, updating 75
  token for library repository, authorizing 75
  token for user repository, authorizing 75
  user repository, creating 74
  user repository, deleting 74
  user repository images, listing 75
  user repository images, updating 74
REST APIs, Docker Hub 73
restart command 32
root privilege
  about 197
  Docker images, loading 199
  emerging security approaches 199
  non-root containers 197, 198
  security implications 199
  trusted user control 197
RUN instruction 49-51

S

Secure Shell (SSH) daemon 175
Secure Sockets Layer (SSL) 80
security, Docker container
  root privilege 197
Security-Enhanced Linux (SELinux)
  about 199
  benefits 201-203
  for container security 199, 200
security features, Docker container
  about 194
  resource accounting and control 196, 197
  resource isolation 195
service computing (SC) 138
SIGKILL signal 30
SIGTERM signal 30
Storage Area Network (SAN) 179

Thank you for buying
Learning Docker

About Packt Publishing

Packt, pronounced 'packed', published its first book, *Mastering phpMyAdmin for Effective MySQL Management*, in April 2004, and subsequently continued to specialize in publishing highly focused books on specific technologies and solutions.

Our books and publications share the experiences of your fellow IT professionals in adapting and customizing today's systems, applications, and frameworks. Our solution-based books give you the knowledge and power to customize the software and technologies you're using to get the job done. Packt books are more specific and less general than the IT books you have seen in the past. Our unique business model allows us to bring you more focused information, giving you more of what you need to know, and less of what you don't.

Packt is a modern yet unique publishing company that focuses on producing quality, cutting-edge books for communities of developers, administrators, and newbies alike. For more information, please visit our website at www.packtpub.com.

Writing for Packt

We welcome all inquiries from people who are interested in authoring. Book proposals should be sent to author@packtpub.com. If your book idea is still at an early stage and you would like to discuss it first before writing a formal book proposal, then please contact us; one of our commissioning editors will get in touch with you.

We're not just looking for published authors; if you have strong technical skills but no writing experience, our experienced editors can help you develop a writing career, or simply get some additional reward for your expertise.

Orchestrating Docker

ISBN: 978-1-78398-478-7   Paperback: 154 pages

Manage and deploy Docker services to containerize applications efficiently

1. Set up your own Heroku-like PaaS by getting accustomed to the Docker ecosystem.

2. Run your applications on development machines, private servers, or the cloud, with minimal cost of a virtual machine.

3. A comprehensive guide to the smooth management and development of Docker containers and its services.

Kali Linux Cookbook

ISBN: 978-1-78328-959-2   Paperback: 260 pages

Over 70 recipes to help you master Kali Linux for effective penetration security testing

1. Recipes designed to educate you extensively on the penetration testing principles and Kali Linux tools.

2. Learning to use Kali Linux tools, such as Metasploit, Wire Shark, and many more through in-depth and structured instructions.

3. Teaching you in an easy-to-follow style, full of examples, illustrations, and tips that will suit experts and novices alike.

Please check **www.PacktPub.com** for information on our titles

Linux Shell Scripting Cookbook

Second Edition

ISBN: 978-1-78216-274-2   Paperback: 384 pages

Over 110 practical recipes to solve real-world shell problems, guaranteed to make you wonder how you ever lived without them

1. Master the art of crafting one-liner command sequence to perform text processing, digging data from files, backups to sysadmin tools, and a lot more.

2. And if powerful text processing isn't enough, see how to make your scripts interact with the web-services like Twitter, Gmail.

3. Explores the possibilities with the shell in a simple and elegant way - you will see how to effectively solve problems in your day to day life.

Jenkins Continuous Integration Cookbook

ISBN: 978-1-84951-740-9   Paperback: 344 pages

Over 80 recipes to maintain, secure, communicate, text, build, and improve the software development process with Jenkins

1. Explore the use of more than 40 best of breed plugins.

2. Use code quality metrics, integration testing through functional and performance testing to measure the quality of your software.

3. Get a problem-solution approach enriched with code examples for practical and easy comprehension.

Please check **www.PacktPub.com** for information on our titles